Cowboys and Caudillos

Cowboys and Caudillos:
Frontier Ideology of the Americas

Tom R. Sullivan

Bowling Green State University Popular Press
Bowling Green, Ohio 43403

Contents

Prefatory Note

Whenever a published translation of a work has been available I have used, in my references, that translation. Some works, such as *Facundo,* have been translated but the translations were not available. Quotations from such works are my own translations. If a translator does not appear in the list of works cited then I am responsible. In order to conserve space I have given quotations only in English.

A version of Chapter II first appeared in *Southwest Review.* Chapter III appeared in *Studies in Latin American Popular Culture.*

I want to thank the University of Puerto Rico for giving me a sabbatical leave to work on this book. Most of all, I want to thank Joy, my loving wife, for her tolerance and support.

"--Oyendo igual sonsonete toda la vida no hay remedio hasta el morir, nada hay que hacer, mas que conformarse con esperar el bien de Dios cruzados de brazos." Agustin Yáñez, *Las tierras flacas*. Mexico City: Editorial Joaquin Mortiz, S.A. 1962, page 115.

"Listening to the same old story all one's life—there's no escape til we die. All we can do is fold our arms, waiting patiently for God's will to be done." Agustin Yáñez, *The Lean Lands*. Trans. Ethel Brinton. Austin: University of Texas Press, 1968, page 102.

Chapter I
The Function of Frontier Narratives

Narrative Sequence and Causality

Narratives explain. A story is a sequence of apparently causally related events. No matter how the story is told or in what medium, the apparent causal relationship between events, explicitly or implicitly, explains conditions when the story ends. Whether told in the traditional temporal pattern, wherein one thing follows another chronologically, or less directly, wherein events are subsumed within the psychology of a narrator, or elliptically, with events related inferentially, the reader or listener or viewer, in order to make sense of what he has experienced, reconstructs what appears to be a causally linked series of events. Because one event causes another—or at least precedes another and thus implies causality— narratives become forms of explanations.

People use stories to explain their behavior. Different behavior requires different stories, which is to say that different stories rationalize different behavior. No claim can be made to the originality of these large assumptions, but since they are assumptions upon which this book builds they should be stated at the beginning.

Most Latin American frontier stories, which explain Latin American experience on frontiers, differ from Anglo American frontier stories. Not surprisingly, the dominant frontier ideology in Latin America differs from the dominant frontier ideology in Anglo America. In Anglo America frontiers often precede expansion; in Latin America frontiers often limit growth. In the five centuries since the discovery of the New World, Anglo America has expanded, both territorially and economically. During those same centuries, Latin America, subjected to the power of first Spain and then England and finally the United States, have suffered economically and, in spite of outward migration in recent years, nations have not expanded territorially. A study of the stories having to do with frontiers may contribute to an explanation of developmental differences.

To be sure, all this suggests that fictions precede history, and surely this will offend many historians. It would be preposterous to claim that the ideas people communicate through narratives generate history. Narratives, and the ideologies they promote and sustain, work in conjunction with economic, geographic, political, traditional and, no doubt, accidental causes to create history. This book may seem to ignore

1

much which frontier historians deem essential to any discussion of how nations have developed. If it slights some aspects of history, and it surely does, it does so in order to focus upon one way in which culture and history intertwine.

This book examines patterns for frontier ideology in narratives. Some of the narratives were chosen for examination because they have been widely accepted by many people for many years. Others were selected because they offer critical commentary upon widely accepted narratives— and the patterns of thought communicated therein—by making what is implicit in those narratives explicit and thus subject to examination and consideration. To make the patterns found in fictional texts more readily apparent, the study refers to the context provided by primary historical sources as well as interpretive commentary by historians of the two cultures. Selected texts from both of the Americas are examined as they reflect frontier ideology or provide commentaries upon that ideology. In general, texts are not considered esthetically desirable or undesirable, although individual works which violate expectations established by widely distributed fictions are given more detailed commentary than those which faithfully follow a *formula*. Formulaic works are treated as a group with but brief examinations of specific titles.

Narratives, Belief, and Literature

No study of narratives about frontier life in the New World could pretend to be encyclopedic. Many narratives not treated at length in this study will come immediately to mind to someone familiar with the topic. Rómulo Gallegos' *Doña Barbara*, Owen Wister's *The Virginian*, Ricardo Güiraldes' *Don Segundo Sombra*, and A.B. Guthrie Jr.'s *The Big Sky* are but a few of the titles now mentioned only in passing which many would expect to see treated at length in a book dealing with New World frontier narratives. Readers familiar with frontier fiction of either culture will think of many other works not included in this study.

On the other hand, many ephemeral works receive considerable attention. Such ephemeral works, or, in other words, popular works, provide highly coherent patterns by which a cultural group explains itself to itself, reaffirms beliefs, and standardizes behavior. Walter de la Mare, a popular poet for a long time, rather elegantly noted that "...popularity is often little more than the smile that comes into the face of a generation seated before its favorite author with palm outstretched, asking not for a bluntly truthful delineation of its fortune or accomplishments, but for a dose of artful flattery" (33). However cynical such a concept of popularity may be, one cannot help but agree that a very good way to make people feel positive about themselves is to tell them good things about themselves, preferably good, familiar truths which can be easily understood and fit comfortably within their view of the world.

Indeed, popular literature, according to Umberto Eco, relies for its appeal on what he labels the principle of redundancy, for it is redundant to tell someone something he or she already believes. "The popular story," he writes, "based on the triumph of information, represents the preferred food for a society which lives among messages charged with redundancy: [it communicates] the sense of tradition, the norms of associated living, the moral principles, the operative rules for valid behavior...everything-...which the social system emits to its members..."(Eco 285). The appeal, Eco tells us, of formulaic stories lies in the fact that "the reader encounters again...that which he already knows, that which he desires to know again..." (283).

Popular literature—in a contemporary, mediated, environment—plays the role traditional narrative, told in traditional ways, played in the past. Although Professor Eco laments the displacement of autochthonous literature by narratives produced by the entertainment industry, he acknowledges that even those narratives "...reflect the implicit pedagogy of a system and function to reinforce existing myths and values" (299).

In fact, Professor Eco seems to underestimate the power of autochthonous traditions. The traditions of frontier narratives in the New World suggest that if the commercial machinery that orders certain narratives to be distributed ignored traditions of the people to whom they wished to sell their products, they would probably have a difficult time making any money. Popular frontier stories of both Anglo and Latin America sustain elements from the cultures from which they have developed. Those elements, in turn, help to sustain the stories, even if those stories are the products of publishing firms and film studios whose primary goal is to make a lot of money.

It will be convenient to have a working definition of *popular*. In Spanish *popular* refers to autochthonous, or folk, art. In English *popular* refers to widely distributed and enjoyed music, film, narrative, comics, clothing, and other, almost always ephemeral, artifacts and activities. Most popular works are intended to attract a mass audience. On the other hand, many serious artists do not expect their work to be enjoyed by such an audience. In this work, *popular* will be used in its English sense, even when referring to works consumed in Spanish.

At any rate, if one wants to understand what many people believe, one way is to study the beliefs communicated by the narratives those people consume. Some very serious people might object. Literary study, they might argue, should not be concerned with such easy, familiar material as widely consumed popular narratives. If proper historians are offended by the suggestion that literature helps to create history then surely proper literary scholars will be offended by inclusion in a literary study material they would never consider to be literature. Literature worthy of study, many scholars affirm, appeals to people of intellect and taste.

Such scholars narrow the study of literature. Their view, usually based on the worn metaphor of taste, deserves considerable condemnation because it impedes sensible study. It eliminates from the study of literature much of the material from which reasonable judgments can be made about what groups of people believe and why they behave the way they behave. It eliminates from the study of literature knowledge of the literary conventions taken from popular literature which many serious artists use—or abuse. It eliminates from the study of literature a sense of the breadth and power of images and associated ideologies which serious artists examine in their work. It divorces the study of serious literature from the context of conventions and ideologies formed by images disseminated by popular literature.

Perhaps that is why popular narratives often interest and disturb serious artists. They see in the clichés of such narrative old truths rounded into falsehood by overuse. Often they are stirred to make troublesome variations with the familiar in their need to tell stories that require readers to consider new versions of truth. The Russian formalist, Viktor Shklovsky, described what serious writers do with highly conventional narrative patterns. As Shklovsky put it, they *defamiliarize* such narrative (Jameson 53). In this process the characteristics of a predictable, ritualistic narrative are turned over, examined, shifted about and used by the artist to reveal unexpected realities about the society that consumes such narratives as well as about individual readers, unexpected truths that are usually as undesirable as they are unexpected. Unlike the cook who spices up an old recipe, making it better for some and for others worse, literary *defamiliarization* is more often than not unpleasant for true lovers of a particular narrative kind. Serious literature often makes us think about what we accept as truth, about the ideology such truths are based in and about the implications such ideologies have for behavior, while popular narrative reaffirms what we accept as truth. Serious narrative often makes us see that those 'mere entertainments' with which we have numbed our minds have been entertaining because they appeal to attitudes which we seldom really examine and which, for comfort's sake, are often best left unexamined.

But whether our experience with it is pleasant or unpleasant, that literature which is labeled serious sometimes depends for its existence on conventional elements from the fossilized, rigidly coherent, highly abstract stories we see and/or read when we indulge ourselves at bedtime with a popular novel or our favorite old television program. Popular literature often provides a fundamental narrative pattern which serious works examine. Without knowledge of the narrative conventions from popular narratives and the beliefs they depend upon, the student of literature may see the narrative by the serious artist as arbitrary, unrelated to the psychology and social life of a mass audience. Without knowledge of the way popular literature inscribes and transmits the images and their associated ideologies favored by the majority of viewers and readers, the student of serious literature may not understand the extent to which the phenomenon examined by the serious artist has its roots in the life of the masses. Serious literature and popular literature, often closely related, should at times, be studied together, especially when the works studied deal with a theme—such as the frontier—basic to the way people live and the way their countries develop.

Jacques Ellul, in *The Humiliation of the Word,* reinforces what Professor Eco tells us about popular literature. Most of the popular literature considered herein consists of image literature, of comics, films, or of written works based on a genre—the Western—familiar in image literature. The image, Ellul tells us, "...is always in conformity with the *doxa* (opinion)...[The image is] especially an influence toward conformity....Images never reinforce anything but conformity to the dominant *doxa*. Only the word troubles the waters" (26). According to Ellul, the word—"the creator, founder, and producer of truth"—the word that troubles the most with its unsocial drive to express truth is the spoken word, for the spoken word not only invites interchange between speaker and listener, an interchange which can qualify and refine meaning, but also because the spoken word comes directly from an individual, not from the collective unconscious of a community which seldom examines the meaning communicated by the images it accepts (23). Popular film, popular comics, and many generic popular novels, usually dependent upon accepted images, nurture the abstractions of the accepted *doxa*. The novelist as artist, with his individual vision, examines the abstractions communicated by images with his own words. The words of the novelist as artist invite reflection, a form of response suppressed by the image. The words of the novelist as artist seek to violate accepted patterns for the imagination.

This book will first examine the frontier experience as presented in popular, widely distributed narratives of the Anglo culture in the New World. Popular, widely distributed narratives of the Hispanic cultures of the New World will next be given the same treatment. Then the way serious authors have examined the same experience, reacting to or using the patterns for thought found in popular narrative, will be described. Finally, the result will be a global description of the differences between the frontier experience in the two cultures and how those different experiences have helped sustain different kinds of frontier literature as well as different kinds of development and behavior.

Frontier Heroes, Space and Order

An introduction to a discussion of New World frontiers in fiction must include two concepts peculiar to New World frontiers—newness and space. But however new the space in the New World was, there were old patterns for imagining what that space should be like and what it should become. When Europeans arrived they saw a world they had never known. First they saw new geography and new space. Later they imagined how it could, and would, be filled with 'real' civilization and 'real' culture—their own civilization and culture that seemed to them to be the culmination of the historical process, and thus the ideal to be aspired to by all (O'Gorman 97).

When Columbus first discovered the islands in the Caribbean he was convinced that he was just offshore from Asia, or, in the case of Cuba, that he had actually found the mainland with all its fabled riches (O'Gorman 30). He looked at the new land and could only see Asia. That is what he had set out to find. That is what he had imagined he would find. America had not been invented, so how could he have expected to find America (O'Gorman 32-33)? Columbus' preconceptions were very hard to displace; it is difficult for facts to violate the imagination. Not until Amerigo Vespucci actually explored the coast of the mainland was it determined that the old concept of a tripartite world, of Europe, Africa and Asia as the whole of the universe, was wrong. Not until then could America be born to European minds as the New World (O'Gorman 71-72).

Once the New World had been identified as new (not Asia) by Vespucci, it had but a geographical existence. It had no history for the European and thus no identity. Once identified as not Asia, the New World had to be imagined (O'Gorman 82). The early maps iconographically reflect the beginning of a historical identity for the New World, an identity assigned by Spaniards and Portuguese. The figure on the maps representing Europe was dressed in symbols of royalty, of domination in religion, art, and industry. Asia was identified by a figure dressed in exotic luxury, while Africa was demonstrably the land of slaves. America's signs were a horn of plenty (indicating possibilities for material exploitation) and a naked man, perhaps suggesting no clear identity, a mere promise, or possibility, in the cultural order (O'Gorman 88). If they imagined that nakedness as savagery, bestiality, as an absence of soul, then the technologically more sophisticated Europeans could imagine the space of the New World as a place where European ownership could be asserted and the Natives used to extract riches. If that naked form on the old maps suggested a human being, formed in the image of God just like the European, then the space could be imagined as a place for the Christian education of the Native American, a place for the development of laws for conduct and construction of cities, all just like education, conduct, and cities in Europe, thus giving the Natives the opportunity to be brought into the process of history. They could become like the European who had 'discovered' them and thereby given them historical existence.

Either way, whether the New World nakedness was imagined as bestiality or possibility for Christian evangelism, European society, and especially, in Latin America, peninsular society provided the model for the incorporation of the New World inhabitants into history. When Europeans in the New World first sought to imagine how they should behave toward Native Americans, when they first tried to imagine how the new space should be filled, how towns and cities should be built, how marriages should be performed, how property should be owned, they looked back to their cultural past for patterns.

One way order had been maintained for centuries in peninsular cultures had been through the system of *caudillaje*. *Caudillaje*, a system of government, a means for giving order to society, depends upon the existence of a *caudillo*. A *caudillo* is, simply put, the most powerful man in a social or political unit. Whether he is a good man or a bad man, benevolent or merciless, politically conservative or liberal, he dictates what will be permitted within the reaches of his power. He is a dictator, but since *caudillaje* has its roots deep within the culture of Spanish America, the more culturally specific term, *caudillo*, seems preferable to the more generic term, *dictator*.

A *caudillo* usually dominates a large area, a state or a nation. On the local level, the term *cacique*, a word taken from the Taino and Arawak Native Americans of the Caribbean, refers to the dominant man. As one writer has put it, "whereas a cacique is a ruler among men, a caudillo is a ruler among caciques..." (Hamill 10). He, or in a few instances she, imposes order upon disorderly social conditions.

The New World provided a ready seed bed for the growth of a dependent relationship between the leader of a community and the people in the community. When the Spaniards arrived in Mexico, the Aztecs had "established in the valley of Anáhuac, where Mexico City is now, in the thirteenth century, a confederation of three or four major tribes. The direction of military operations was entrusted to the Aztecs. The military chieftain (*tlacatecuhtli*), whom the Spaniards called emperor, exercised functions similar to those originally accruing to the *imperator* in Rome. He was not king, yet he held office for life; and the office was elective, not hereditary. The civil power was in the hands of another chieftain (*cihuacóhuatl*), and both the civil authorities and the military appear to have depended ultimately on the council (*tlatocan*) of representatives of the regional groups (*culpulis*) derived from local clans..." (Henriquez Ureña 13).

The Spaniards found the hierarchical relationship between military, civil, and clan convenient for the imposition of order. Certainly *caudillaje* found new strength in the immensity of a continent where the king of Spain had difficulty in making his authority felt in all places (Chevalier 37). New World space was too immense to allow the Spaniards to impress their civilization, their order, without dividing that space into smaller governmental units. Thus, as one historian has put it, "Given geographic isolation and the vastness of the region, the scattered power nuclei, controlled by caciques, were fundamental to the emergence of a national caudillo" (Hamill 10). With the system of *caciques* and their more powerful superiors, *caudillos,* in place, the Spaniards found a readily available means of establishing order in the hinterlands and thus a form of dominance over those hinterlands (Chevalier 38). The system of *caudillaje,* useful, exploited, became a part of Latin American culture, the way order was imposed and maintained in the hinterlands.

Because dependence upon *caudillos* to impose and maintain order became a part of the culture of Latin America, it provided the pattern for settlement in that part of the New World. The new men who came to the New World were looking for their fortunes. They were looking for opportunities to be like the rich and powerful in Spain. Many succeeded and became proprietors of estates, with power over vast expanses of land. As in Spain, the "mentality of the great proprietors encouraged the proliferation of personal bonds...they found compensation in the quasi-seignorial prestige that a crowd of men attached to their land and to their person could give to their masters..." (Chevalier 38). As the new men established ownership of space in the new world, they established themselves as *caudillos* of that region.

Various commentators have advanced various reasons for the frequent reincarnations in Latin America of the *caudillo.* An unpleasant rationale for *caudillaje* can be found in the metaphor of development. The word carries with it connotations concerning levels of civilization; to be *developed* is to be civilized; to be *underdeveloped* is to be uncivilized. No less a commentator than Domingo Sarmiento, whose great Argentine novel about *caudillos* will be examined in Chapter VII, advanced what can be called the uncivilized Hispanic theory for *caudillaje.* The Argentine, Sarmiento argued, and by extension all Latin American people, were simply not experienced enough, in 1845, to be truly civilized. Since, according to Sarmiento, under the respectable frock coat of every Argentine one could find a repressed *gaucho,* then the strong hand of the *caudillo* was inevitably necessary, demanded by the nature of the people. Moreover, the repressive and violent methods of the *caudillo* are not simply characteristics of the man, the individual *caudillo,* but of the people themselves, who were not ready for human rights. Human rights, he tells us, are the result of centuries of civilization, and in 1845, the Argentine savage simply hadn't had enough time to learn about them (Sarmiento 142).

Other commentators have attributed the frequency of the *caudillo* in Latin America to educational and political naivité. *"Continuismo* [the practice of allowing a strong man to stay in office indefinitely] has been favored in middle America by just those conditions which nurture dictatorship—and to just the same extent. A high degree of illiteracy, of political inarticulateness and even unconsciousness, of governmental concentration, all make for those expressions of exaggerated personalism of which this legalized perpetuation of control is a form" (Fitzgibbon 145).

Perhaps a more plausible, and certainly a less racist justification for *caudillaje* than some of the above, attributes it to a failure to resolve a conflict between a desire for order, inherent in Spanish culture, and a desire for individualism, inherent in Spanish culture. The desire for order evidently takes precedence when people turn to a *caudillo*. The *caudillo*, who possesses all within his power, expresses the extreme individualism of the people (Lloyd Jones 224-225). Even Sarmiento, who despised two of the most famous Argentine *caudillos*, Juan Manuel Rosas and Juan Facundo Quirago, celebrated the order a strong man could give to a country: "It is a grand and spectacular moment for a country when a vigorous hand takes power of its destiny," he wrote (76). Later, discussing the time when Juan Manuel Rosas took power, he tells us that, "The peaceful citizens expected it [Rosas' rule] as a benediction and an end to the cruel oscillations of two long years....There is a fatal moment in the history of every people and that is when, tired of the struggles between parties, [they] ask above all for repose from [struggle]...even at the expense of liberty or of the ends which they desire; this is the moment in which tyrants form dynasties and empires" (183).

There may be a much more homely reason for the frequent reversion to *caudillos* in Latin America. The form of government Spaniards had known was a monarchy. They were Catholic. Both Catholicism and monarchy suggest an order among human beings according to rank. Perhaps because their form of government and their religion suggested a hierarchical relationship among the human family, Latin Americans imagined that in the New World social units should look to a strong man for direction, just as a son should look to his father for guidance.

Certainly *caudillaje* did not depend upon mere legal ties to Spain. After the wars of emancipation in the early nineteenth century, *caudillos* appeared everywhere. Without the Spanish state, without the traditional aristocracy and given the retreat of the Church, a power vacuum existed. When peace returned, the new men usually kept the power the luck of war and circumstance had given them (Chevalier 39). The people wanted peace, justice, and order. Frequently they looked to *caudillos* to give them what they wanted.

The system of *caudillaje* enabled the Spanish, and later independent *caudillos,* to impose order in the hinterlands of the New World. After independence, one might no longer have a King, a council, or even a viceroy, but one still needed to imagine that somewhere an individual had sufficient strength and wisdom to direct human secular activity just as the priest directed human religious activity. While new nations were being born, new governments established and, in far too many cases, destroyed and established over and over again, men and women needed social order. They found that order in the strength of a local or regional strong man, a *caudillo.*

Caudillos provided order in a world of disorder, and it is probable that people found some kind of law, even the personal law of one man, better than no law at all. *Caudillos* brought order to New World frontiers in Latin America. *Caudillos* were the heroes of Latin American frontiers.

In 1620, when the pilgrims landed at Plymouth Rock, they also perceived space and newness, but the way they imagined political organization within that space was far different from Latin American frontiersmen who preceded them in the New World. The Puritan faith of Anglo Americans was far more individualistic than the Catholicism of Latin Americans. Puritans believed that through work in this world the individual could demonstrate his virtue. Through stewardship of God's gifts he could acquire wealth and importance in the community, evidence of spiritual as well as of worldly value. On the other hand, if an individual were idle and did not attend to duty, such idleness would deprive that person of worldly goods and reveal to all evidence of spiritual, as well as worldly, poverty.

When the Puritans encountered Native Americans on the North American frontier they encountered people with very little wealth and with little inclination to till the soil and make it fruitful. Moreover, Native Americans were obviously not Christian. The Puritans surmised a third way of seeing the new people they had found, neither that of Father Bartolomé de las Casas, who saw the denizens of the New World as human beings for whom Europeans were sent to teach Christianity, nor that of Father Juan Ginés de Sepúlveda, who saw Native Americans as beasts without souls. For the Puritans, Native Americans were human, but for some reason God had withheld Christian Grace from them. To be sure, later Americans, such as Benjamin Franklin, were racists who believed, as most people of his time, that Native Americans were "barbarous tribes of savages that delight in war and take pride in murder" (Hunt 46). Still, such savages, although far beneath the rank of white people, and not worthy of owning property, were at least of the same species as other human beings.

Since, as the Puritans would have it, every individual had to be responsible for his or her own salvation, the Puritan community could scarcely grant Grace to Native Americans. In fact, since it was generally understood that Native Americans not only did not benefit from God's Grace but were actually in the service of Satan, too much contact with them could cost one his or her own salvation.

Captivity Stories, told in sermons and later by story tellers, reaffirmed for Anglo Americans the way to imagine relations with the people of the New World. Later, Anglo Americans needed more space. To take it from Native Americans, who had obviously not cultivated the earth, seemed scarcely a sin, seen in the light of Puritan religious beliefs. Moreover, as R.A. Billington has argued, Anglo Americans were always a restless lot, eager to improve themselves, and the land really did seem unused according to Puritan standards for use (Zea 219). However, perhaps to reinforce their belief in the rectitude of their behavior and/or to explain it to themselves, new heroes were required. The survivalist frontiersman, first a trapper and a hunter but later to become the cowboy, whose restless, individualistic nature led him ever outward to new space, but whose loyalties remained firmly fixed with the culture he left behind, embodied the new hero. Such heroes were men who could make new space safe for colonists, who could create the order Anglo culture required in the New World.

Unlike the *caudillo*, the cowboy seldom acquired official political status; nevertheless, like the *caudillo*, the cowboy, at least according to the way Anglo Americans came to imagine history, imposed the order on the frontier that was necessary for development according to European standards.

The Frontier, a Definition

At least one problem remains for this study of New World frontier ideology. *Frontier*, so rhetorically abused as a word in the United States, may have very little real meaning left for many people. Frederick Jackson Turner defined the frontier in Anglo America as the "furthest edge of settlement." In his essay the word *settlement* referred to the colonization by European people or their descendants of territory formerly inhabited by Native Americans. Turner used the word as it was commonly understood, as a euphemism for a process of nation building that seldom provided just compensation to the people that preceded the Anglo American in North America, for to *settle* a territory suggested improvement of that land as it was taken from the control of savages. Environmentalists today might question whether such *settlement* has always led to improvement.

Not only did *settle* become a euphemism, it became a jingoistic rallying cry for outward movement. The word calls forth the image of the hero creating the home of the free and the brave, along with the image of the new country bounded on the west by a moving line being pushed across the breadth of the United States, on one side nomadic bands of culturally and politically disorganized people, on the other organized, stable, *settled* and orderly citizens.

Of course political and commercial interests exploit the word to further good, bad, and indifferent causes, and in the process frequently reinforce its jingoistic connotations. We have had, to mention those uses which come most immediately to mind, President Kennedy's New Frontier, the Last Frontier (in Alaska's most recent tourist advertisements) the Urban Frontier, the Frontiers of Space, the Frontiers of Science, as well as people working on the frontiers of various occupations. Advertisers and rhetoricians of all sorts link products and activities with something thought to be peculiar to the United States of America, the American Frontier Spirit. Indeed, to be critical, even in the literary sense of analysis and examination, of anything associated with the American Frontier Spirit, seems to some to smack of opposition to the basic values upon which the United States rests its claim to greatness.

The Spanish cognate of *frontier, frontera,* denotes *border,* a line or frequently a river or some other geographical phenomenon where the control of territory is under one power on one side and of another on the other. *Frontera* doesn't seem to have taken on the rhetorical freight that *frontier* carries. Alistair Hennessy, in *The Frontier in Latin American History,* gives the English word a twist when he describes mining frontiers, cattle frontiers, agricultural frontiers, rubber frontiers as well as, of course, political and cultural frontiers in Latin America. His study of Latin American frontiers conjures images of numerous circles constantly appearing and disappearing on a map of Latin America as men go from the centers to the hinterlands, establish an industry such as mining, exhaust the mines, as at Potosi in Bolivia, then return to the centers of their countries or to Spain to live on what they earned while on the frontier.

Thus the words, *frontier* and *frontera* look like exact cognates but like so many cognates they connote quite different things within the cultures and the languages in which they exist. Such differences would seem to make the concepts of the *frontier* and the *frontera* impossible to compare. Such would be the case were it not for the reflection and study of Jorge Mañach in *Teoría de la frontera [Theory of the Frontier],* in which he defined *frontier/frontera* in a way which encompasses— or circumvents—problems caused by the connotations of the word in English and the more denotative Spanish meaning. He called a *frontera/ frontier* a point of contiguity and conflict between two groups. He thus speaks of *frontiers* (hereafter only used in English) within cities and of course of frontiers within and between countries. With such a definition those circles of space—on the map of Latin America described by Hennessy—share with the line of conquest the word conjures in the imaginations of many North American people, the denotation of a point or a series of points where different groups of people suffer or enjoy contiguity and conflict. It is in this sense that the word *frontier* will be used in the following comparison of some of the frontier stories of the two dominant cultures in the New World.

Frontiers and Development

An hypothesis about frontier ideology in the New World underlies both the selection of what is treated herein as well as the treatment of what is selected. After study of encyclopedic literary histories, after talk with friends who are specialists in Latin American literature, after the usual work with card catalogues and bibliographies, after reading as many primary works as possible and after living fifteen years in Latin America—some may wonder why in the world it took so long—the hypothesis emerged: widely disseminated Latin American narratives reinforce a centralist set of ideas related to frontier life. Such narratives reinforce *caudillaje,* or dependence upon a strong man to establish and maintain order. Such men are at the center of their social and political unit. Their power promises social organization at the center. In the most common frontier fictions of the Hispanic world those who venture too far from the center of their social unit, from family, society, and *caudillo,* are likely to lose their way, to become savage, to require the correction and assistance of central authority if they are to avert a sad or perhaps a degenerate life. To be alone in the hinterlands of the Latin American world is to be potentially pathetic. Contrary to conventional wisdom, which affirms that Latin America tends to fragment, rather than to unify, Latin Americans depict in their stories a centripetal and implosive frontier ideology, one which promotes unity beneath the rule of a *caudillo.*

Conversely, widely disseminated Anglo American narratives foster expansionist ideas about frontiers. Certainly such an idea about Anglo American narratives is far from new. Richard Slotkin, for example, performed an admirable and exciting scholarly task in his book, *Regeneration Through Violence* (1973), as he traced the evolution of Anglo American frontier narratives from stories about captives to stories about cowboys. He, among others, has shown how Anglo American frontier stories depict heroes who venture forth, men who are leaders, pathfinders, explorers who make conquered land safe for peaceful colonists. In such stories to be alone on the frontier is to be potentially heroic. Anglo Americans depict in their frontier stories a centrifugal, explosive frontier vision.

This comparative study of narratives from the two cultures may not illuminate much that is new for specialists in Latin American or Anglo American frontier literature and history. The book breaks new territory in comparing the narratives, and the ideologies communicated, from the two cultures. Such a comparison can contribute to understanding different patterns for development.

Chapter II
L'Amour's Explosive Action Packed Western
for Anglo America

The frontier fiction of the United States, the Western, provides many people of the United States with a pattern for processing information about their nation's history. For many, popular frontier fictions provide images which enable them to identify with the positive aspects of that history. Images taken from film, television, and best-selling fictions, supposedly about life on the frontier of the nineteenth century, reassure those people that the cars they drive, the clothes they wear, the food they eat, the cigarettes they smoke, even the perfume they put on their skin, communicate their self-sufficiency—a most desirable trait for a frontiersman. The same images identify them as members of a community in which social and political issues are often judged in the light of the same idealized historical vision of the frontier. Unfortunately, as Jacque Ellul has it, images provide "prefabricated certainties...[and reassurance for] behavior guaranteed not to require choices" (34).

The novels of Louis L'Amour are the most common current print media for the images of the United States frontier of settlement. L'Amour died on 10 June 1988. He was eighty years old. According to his obituary in *The New York Times* of 13 June 1988, there are nearly 200 million copies of his 101 novels now in print. Such acceptance is a measure of the congruence between his version of the frontier fiction and the version of the frontier many people (obviously, many millions of people) find most pleasing today.

A Louis L'Amour Western inculcates the principle that violence must precede peace. When a strong man confronts evil he must use his guns or his fists, he must "read them from the Book," as it is frequently put, suggesting a kind of Old Testament justice. In *Sackett* (1961) Ange Kerry, later to become Tell Sackett's wife, is at first horrified by his violence. She, like others "who live sheltered or quiet lives, away from violent men, have no idea how they have to be dealt with" (83). In *The Haunted Mesa* (1987) Mike Raglan, the hero, having been assaulted by two men and having, of course, beaten them up, explains to the Sheriff, "I read them from The Book" (226). In the same fiction the narrator argues that the United States triumphed over Mexico during the war

15

with Mexico because Americans had the constitutional right to carry arms and most Americans knew how to use them. Only some women and city men are opposed to armed violence. Fist fighting, wrestling and martial arts are used as frequently as guns. Johannes Verne, in *The Lonesome Gods* (1983), while only ten years old, must fight the school bully, Rad Huber.

He [the bully] was larger in every way, and much heavier, but how much did he know? He had his fists up ready to strike, and mine were up too; then suddenly I dove, grasping his ankle with both hands and throwing my weight against his knee as I jerked up on the ankle. He toppled over on his back.

Instantly, holding his ankle in my right armpit, I stepped across his body, half-turning him toward the ground. Then I dropped to a sitting position on his buttocks, facing the opposite way. The Indians had taught me this, and I knew I had only to put more pressure on his ankle and his hip would be dislocated.

I leaned back a little, and he cried out. Fraser [the teacher] had turned and was coming toward us. Out on the street Jacob Finney had come up with my horse and his. He sat his saddle, watching.

Meghan stood with the other girls, their faces showing excitement and shock.

"Let him up!" Mr. Fraser ordered.

"Ask him if he will let me alone. I want no more trouble."

"Will you let him alone, Rad?" Fraser asked.

"I'll kill him!"

I leaned back again, and this time he screamed. Then he said, "No! No! Get off me! I won't do nothin'!" (149-150)

In *Ride the Dark Trail* (1972), Logan Sackett is pressed into a fist fight with a bully who has accused him of having stolen horses. The bully is well known as a fighter, and many people are afraid of him. Logan gives the bully a severe whipping, not only punishing him physically, but verbally scolding him afterwards.

The villains are always clearly villainous in such situations. Rad Huber in *The Lonesome Gods* has beaten the young Johannes unmercifully before school and harassed him throughout the day, and the bully Logan Sackett wallops certainly merits his punishment. The images the fights conjure reaffirm what readers who have learned the frontier ideology of the United States already know—that courage and physical prowess were required to establish Anglo-American order and decency on the frontier. As the reader follows the fights in print he learns nothing ideologically new, but instead enjoys a familiar sense of communal moral triumph.

A transient hero is basic to the traditional Western. At the end of a frontier fiction Hawkeye or Shane or any one of their thousands of counterparts, such as Gene Autry, Roy Rogers, or Hopalong Cassidy, should be seen disappearing into the far mountains or prairies, alone, or perhaps with their soon to vanish faithful Native American friend—

Tonto or Chingachgook, or their equally anachronistic comic side kick, an old trapper such as Gabby Hayes or an inept yokel such as Smiley Burnette. Although the image does not make anything explicit, and the viewer, under the sway of attitudes never examined, is not aware, the hero takes into the wilderness the narcissistic ideal of the self-sufficient, self-reliant, totally masculine individual. Behind him he leaves a peaceful community, with women, children, and schools. The convention has been underscored by repeated use in thousands of narratives. Yet, in many of the fictions of Louis L'Amour, the hero is in search of a community which he will not only protect with his violent frontier skills, but later live in, where he will *settle* to a life with a wife, children, and town council meetings.

Thus a L'Amour hero often not only fights and kills to establish a community patterned on European cultural systems but also often remains to live in the community, even if, frequently, the reader only receives in the closing pages of the fiction hints of the hero's life as a man of the community. Nevertheless, the change from the transient hero to a potential, at least, settled colonist suggests that the hero embodies values associated with an expansionist frontier ideal as well as the capacity to colonize necessary to actualize that ideal.

Johannes Verne, the hero of *The Lonesome Gods* (1983), offers a good example of the ambiguity of a hero committed to town-building and community life while, at the same time, emotionally drawn to life in the wilderness. Johannes, taken to California by his father who is dying of tuberculosis, then left to die in the desert by his maternal grandfather, a *Californio* or Mexican settler who has been shamed by his daughter's marriage to Johannes' father, an Anglo American without name or position. Johannes grows to manhood in the care, first, of Native Americans and, later, Miss Nesselrode, a Russian immigrant lady of considerable cultural accomplishment. Miss Nesselrode sees possibilities for growth and financial reward as Los Angeles develops under the influence of the energetic Yankees who are taking over the town. Johannes works in her book shop, reads her books, and appears to be an industrious town boy, willing to study and work hard in order to get ahead. He falls in love with Meghan, the daughter of an important sea captain with high social connections, and, at the end of the fiction, the reader may surmise that he will marry Meghan and continue enjoying town building with Miss Nesselrode and her friends—and getting rich while at it. Yet throughout the fiction the reader is reminded of Johannes' love for the desert acquired while living with Native Americans. Johannes endures a climactic struggle for survival in the desert—for which he is better equipped than any of the villains due to his life with Native Americans. So, although it seems fair to surmise that Johannes will work to build the town of Los Angeles, it seems also fair to surmise that he will continue to love the desert and the life of adventure therein.

L'Amour uses point of view to reinforce the hero's status within the community. In many L'Amour novels the hero/narrator, absolutely reliable, speaks in the first person, and sometimes attests to his authenticity by his back country dialect. Moreover, he is a veritable fount of down-to-earth folk—and therefore redundant—wisdom as he makes frequent use of formulaic language. For example, men who are loyal to a ranch "ride for the brand," men who have experienced a great deal have been "up the crick and over the mountain," old men are "old curly wolves from the high country," and a real man's coffee should, invariably, be "black and bitter." Real men, as has been noted, "do not back up from a fight," nor do they "owe others for their keep." "One thing I'd learned over the years," Tell Sackett moralizes in *The Sackett Brand* (1965), "never to waste time moaning about what couldn't be helped. If a body can do something, fine—he should do it. If he can't then there's no use fussing about it until he *can* do something" (23).

Some L'Amour heroes may be poorly educated, as the examples of dialect above attest, but they often aspire to education and, when possible, as in *Sackett* (1961), borrow books in order to study. Conn Drury, the hero in *Kiowa Trail* (1964), demonstrates that he has read Thomas Carlyle. Johannes Verne, in *The Lonesome Gods* (1983), reads the works of Bulwer-Lytton, the nineteenth century British novelist. In *Treasure Mountain* (1972), the narrator hero, Tyrel Sackett, unlettered though he may be, pauses to tell the reader the etymology of the word *Dixie* as a place name for the South. The heroes signify by such literary and semantic knowledge that, although they may be rugged survivalists, they are civilized men who can be trusted not to deny their Anglo American heritage.

Such narrators further demonstrate their union with the community by their knowledge of communal morality. In *Shalako* (1962), the narrator affirms the following generalizations—already a part of general knowledge gleaned from images in film, television, and comic books—about moral life in the West:

> A man in the Western lands was as big as he wanted to be and as good or as bad as he wished. What law existed was local law and it felt no responsibility for the actions of any man when they took place out of its immediate jurisdiction. There were very few border-line cases. Men were good and bad...simply that...the restrictions were few, the chances of concealment almost nonexistent. A man who was bad was boldly bad, and nobody sheltered or protected any man. (10)

On the same page, scarcely fifty words later, we are given the following factual information:

Men in the West rarely rode mares or stallions. There might be exceptions, but they were so scarce as to attract a good deal of attention. They rode geldings because they were less trouble among other horses. (10)

Since we have no reason to doubt the very sensible observation concerning the use of geldings in the Old West, the information authenticates the narrative voice. Because the narrator controls such factual information, we are assured of the reliability of his moral observations concerning his time and place.

Occasionally one is tempted to doubt the verisimilitude. The narrator's observations refer to a past (when men were as good or as bad as they wished) which he is recalling from some indeterminate point afterwards, at the moment of narration, one assumes, in present time. This would require the narrator to be an active and conscious man who has lived well over a century—unusual, to say the least. It is a conventional anachronism in formulaic Westerns; as shall be seen later, Western films frequently mixed wagon and horse transportation with modern trains and automobiles. The convention establishes the morality and behavioral standards presumed to have existed in the Old West as standards for judgment of contemporary events and behavior. In L'Amour's novels the effect is to create a narrative voice absolute in its authority as a spokesman for the past and a judge of the present. The reader who gives him or herself to the fiction must accept that authority: it carries the homely wisdom of family truth. Moreover, the convention enables the traditional ideology of the Western, an ideology which many people accept as the basis for their lives, to adapt to technological change. Cowboy truth prevails even as time goes by, on a train, in automobiles, on airplanes, or carried by microchips. L'Amour's ideology travels easily in time and space.

L'Amour's violence prone heroes often establish a solid social position within their communities and frequently are upwardly mobile. Their movement upward on the social and economic scale underscores the town-building motif, a motif central to many Westerns, whereby the colonization of new territory is acted out and the new space 'discovered' by Anglo Americans filled with law, order, and progress as conceived within Anglo American cultures. In *The Daybreakers* (1960), Orrin and Tyrel Sackett leave their rocky and barren farm in Tennessee in order to find a new home for their aged, pipe-smoking Ma. They settle in New Mexico, fight Native Americans and the chicanery of an Eastern land shark, then create their own estate. Orrin is elected to a variety of political positions, ultimately to the state legislature, while Tyrel serves as town Marshall. In *Sackett* (1971), William Tell Sackett, inspired by the examples of his younger brothers, Orrin and Tyrel (the members of the family reoccur in various novels) starts a town, works a gold mine for a grubstake, discovers a young bride, and begins a respectable, middle class life. The hero of *The Man Called Noon* (1970) begins the novel a fugitive but manages, before the final bullet, to save a ranch made barren by a lawless band, to restore it to its rightful owner, a young woman held captive thereon, and finally to begin a respectable, middle class life with the young woman as his wife. His violent life has not made him a sinner, unworthy of life as a proper neighbor and marriage with the heiress to the ranch, nor does his knowledge of the time of the primordial innocence of the land, a knowledge which enables his survival, make him a saint unsuited for life within the community. He succeeds within the system. He progresses in time while maintaining the values of the community.

However well established within his community a L'Amour frontiersmen may be, he remains a frontiersman, yearning to challenge wilderness in order to find out what is there. Therefore, a L'Amour hero must be a survivalist. He must know which cactus plant will provide food and moisture in the desert. He must know that all desert travel should take place at night. He must know that his horse will be able to smell water long before a man will be able to see water. Armed with such knowledge, presumably learned, directly or indirectly, from Native Americans, he triumphs, not merely over the environment, but over those who for whatever reason oppose his presence in that environment.

As survivalists, L'Amour's heroes acquire great practical knowledge. Since that kind of knowledge enables survival it has greater value in the culture than learning acquired through schools. Such heroes, in spite of those who read Thomas Carlyle and Bulwer-Lytton, live a life of action, not of the mind. Indeed, it is likely that only fools and weaklings will emerge from institutional education, since they will probably not have the survival skills necessary for the frontier. The schoolmaster, Mr. Fraser, in *The Lonesome Gods* (1983), offers a ready example. He doesn't get a shot off in a skirmish with Native Americans, and he doesn't take advantage of opportunities to make money. Instead, he spends an interminable time barely making a living as a teacher while he works on his one presumably great work of scholarship. A L'Amour hero gets on with life in a timely fashion. Action packed scenes wherein violent heroes overcome environmental conditions and uncivil enemies communicate an anti-intellectual attitude inherent in Anglo American culture.

The L'Amour frontiersman triumphs, and his race does, and such economic and social success, confirming and consolidating territorial expansion, demonstrates the will of God. *The Californios* (1974) clearly illustrates such a desire on the part of the Supernatural. The fiction is set in California in 1844, three years before Mexico was required to cede nearly one half of its territory to the United States, but the fiction assumes Anglo American dominance to be an accomplished or at least an inevitable fact. The Californios of the title are Mexicans who have lived their lives under the Mexican flag in California. They are divided into three groups: the good, generally servile old family retainers, such as Jesús Montero who we see, when he is talking to his Anglo American employers, "twisting his hat in his hands," (45) the very image of servility; the bad, who tend to be standard, knife carrying stereotypes, basically indistinguishable one from the other, who work for the Anglo American villain; and the harmless, but socially acceptable, wealthy class who "will not leave the missions or the pueblos," for they "like company and they are not adventurous" (12) and many "still lived in their dreams...a peaceful quiet world secluded from all that lay outside" (126). The third group forms a happy but acquiescent lot, having been conditioned by a climate where "the seasons merged, dreamed one into the other, and what was not done today could be done tomorrow" (127). As usual, such ethnic abstractions simply confirm attitudes the images have already invoked.

On the other hand, the newcomers, the Anglo Americans, were "energetic and accustomed to competition and the drive to succeed," conditioned by life in New England and Northern Europe where "the seasons were short and the air brisk," and where one "had little time to do what needed to be done" (126-127). Such people love the "struggle for existence" and therefore "their coming could not help but bring changes" (126). Obviously, in contrast to the Anglo Americans, who had been culturally and geographically determined to succeed as colonists, the Mexicans were not at all suitable stock for pioneering.

Anglo American pioneers, in fact, perform altruistic service—certainly action a merciful God would warrant—for the Mexicans while colonizing their land. The Mexicans are beset by an Anglo American villain, a man who wants to dominate the territory without regard for Anglo American colonists or their Mexican predecessors. The bad Mexicans are in the service of the villain while the good Mexicans are powerless. Zeke Wooston, the villain, having heard rumors of gold on the ranch of a beautiful widow, Eileen Mulkerin, buys a mortgage on the ranch and tries to foreclose when the mortgage is due. The beautiful widow has two sons, Michael and Sean. Michael, alas, has joined the church and become a man of peace. He counsels his mother to give up rather than confront Wooston. Happily, given the demands of the Western formula plot and the pattern for frontier thought which that formula embodies, the other son, Sean, a man of action, knows that no peace is possible unless a true man adopts violent means for survival. He is joined by three Anglo Americans in the 'showdown' with Wooston's men, three Anglo Americans who know, as does Sean, that it is to no avail on the frontier to have "evidence that will stand in a court of law," and who "ain't figurin' on takin' it [their suspicion that Wooston has stolen their cattle] to no court," because "out yonder in the desert it's a fur piece to the law so we just have to make do" (146).

With knowledge, energy, and skillful use of firepower, the good Anglo Americans overcome the evil Wooston and protect the community, including the lazy Californios. But lest the reader suspect such racial superiority to be merely the result of climatic conditions, he is shown that some kind of divinity favors Anglo Americans in California. Much of the novel consists of an extended camping trip into the mountains undertaken by Sean, his mother Eileen, Mariana (a beautiful Mexican girl from a wealthy, Mexico City family), and Jesús Montero, the faithful family retainer. They are led by a very old, in fact a supernaturally old, Native American called Juan. Juan is not of any of the contemporary tribes of Native Americans, but rather, with lighter skin and more refined facial features, the last of a far more advanced civilization destroyed by an earthquake in the distant past. Apparently L'Amour assumed that his readers would think of lighter skin and refined facial features as images of levels of racial achievement.

Juan knows where his ancient people left gold, and it is in search of this gold—in order to get money to save the ranch—that they undertake the camping expedition. It is quite fortunate for the Mulkerins that they have Juan as a friend. He has judged them and found them worthy, has, in fact, spent considerable time imparting his ancient wisdom to Sean. On the other hand, Juan has had little contact with the Californios since they seldom venture into the mountains where he lives, which suggests yet further evidence that those who venture beyond frontiers are the favorites of destiny.

Juan's wisdom goes beyond simple knowledge about gold; he is in direct contact with people on the "other side," members of his tribe who have died to the observable world but who live on in a parallel, unseen, world. It is from this supernatural source that Juan gets his power, and it is with that power that he blesses Sean, directs him, and even enables him to communicate with the "others."

The hero, Sean, and his people, given such supernatural help, are destined to replace the lazy Californios and to defeat the evil Wooston with his knife wielding hired killers. The message is underscored a final time when, during the night, while everyone is sleeping, a mysterious gift is left—in a container that identifies it with the "others." The mysterious gift is in the form of gold, enough to pay off the mortgage, allowing Sean to marry the lovely Mariana and the process of economic growth, and territorial consolidation, so obviously ordained by supernatural policy, to continue for the progressive Anglo American family.

Nine years after the appearance of *The Californios* L'Amour demonstrated once again—in *The Lonesome Gods* (1983)—that Anglo American expansion into California reflected the will of God. Once again Mexican colonists, or Californios, are either in the employ of villains, or, if upper class, dominated by tradition and unable to join the inevitable, according to L'Amour, process of historical development. They cannot act except to attempt to maintain tradition. They assume that their feudal society will exist forever and they are too lazy to compete with the aggressive Anglo Americans who come into their midst. They seldom venture into the desert and thus do not really do any active colonization. They mortgage their property to the Yankees and, since they do not know how to manage money, soon lose their land. They do not recognize the value of buying land for orchards. They are not good stewards. They lack foresight so they do not realize that Los Angeles will grow and that to own land near the city will be profitable. They live outside while the Yankees march to the tick of the clock.

However, as in *The Californios* (1974), it is the hero's relationship with supernatural beings that assures his success. He is given the power to see ancient Native Americans who have wandered the desert long before contemporary Native Americans appeared. He recognizes the small temples left by the ancient people to these 'lonesome' gods and leaves small rock tributes to them. He is favored by them and that favor enables him to survive.

Colonization, and the expansion of one's territory, is a patriotic duty in a L'Amour novel. Nations that do not expand eventually become decadent. They are likely to be closed societies which do not permit new ideas to enter. As we have seen in *The Californios* (1974) and *The Lonesome Gods* (1983), the closed society of the Mexican period of political domination in California led to its decadence and, eventually, to its collapse. In *The Haunted Mesa* (1987) L'Amour is quite didactic about an expansionist frontier policy as a prerequisite for the survival of a nation and its culture. The hero, Mike Raglan, having gone to 'the other side,' a parallel reality such as that known by Juan in *The Californios* (1974), confronts Zipacna, the strong man who represents the invisible and totally inaccessible government—called The Hand— of the 'other side.' Raglan has this to say to the imperious Zipacna: "The Hand has been wise to exclude outsiders. Over on our side we have a compulsive drive to move into any area that offers opportunity, and your country is dying. It is ripe for a takeover, as you yourself have decided" (338). According to L'Amour, without a compulsive drive to expand, without the will to ignore a frontier if an opportunity exists on the other side, a culture and a nation will die or be so weakened that it will be easily dominated by more energetic people. It is therefore the patriotic duty of a citizen to colonize whatever space, or dimension, that exists, and while so doing to make the space over in the image of the culture to which he or she belongs.

For three decades Louis L'Amour was the most visible and widely published author of contemporary novels about the frontier of the United States. The changes Louis L'Amour made in the traditional pattern for the Western are slight and obviously do not disturb the millions of people who read Westerns. They probably do not find it strange for a hero in a L'Amour fiction to settle down within a social unit he has defended with his guns. In individual terms the L'Amour hero looks for ways to progress economically as he ventures across frontiers. In historical terms economic expansion (as opposed to territorial expansion) has been the preferred method for national growth during the present century.

L'Amour's heroes profess a love for peace, but their lives always involve great violence. Throughout the development of the United States national spokesmen have expressed a love for peace but the history of the nation has been interrupted by violent wars. The ideology of the frontier in the United States, promulgated in our time by the images in the novels of Louis L'Amour, enables readers to resolve such logical opposites. Communication by use of images, their content inscribed by experience with film and television, does not promote logical analysis.

But frontier ideology in the United States does more than provide an irrational resolution of conflicting national characteristics. If the ideology of the frontier, as embodied in the fictions of Louis L'Amour and his many predecessors, fails to endow their readers with the desire to understand themselves in rational ways, it does endow them with the desire to create new technologies, new ways of using human and natural resources in order to 'settle' and develop the Garden of the Lord. If it fails to offer its readers a vision of the life of the mind as a life worthy of emulation, it does foment a work ethic that gets things done. If it has created a restless people, constantly moving from one place to another, with fragmented families and a dearth of tradition, it has enabled some individuals to find freedom to think and act as they wish outside the constrictions of traditional and often conservative social units. Time does not trap many citizens of the United States, and some of that freedom to accept change stems from popular frontier ideology.

Some troublesome facts remain. Louis L'Amour's fictions, enmeshed with the ideology of the frontier as it has developed in the United States, sustain and foment an expansionist mentality which promotes an intrusive foreign policy. Such a policy had its beginnings in Jeffersonian America, when Anglo Americans sought territory presumably in order to provide more land for liberty-loving-farmers. Eventually, according to Michael H. Hunt in *Ideology and U.S. Foreign Policy,* the goal of national greatness, achieved through expansion, was actively pursued as the nation grew. The idea that the United States must continuously struggle to achieve the national greatness it merited became one of the fundamental ideas of Anglo American foreign policy. "'The road to national greatness required unremitting struggle,' so [Theodore] Roosevelt proclaimed...Conflict among nations was natural. The fit would prevail and the weak go down to defeat and extinction. 'All the great masterful races have been fighting races,' he [Theodore Roosevelt] readily concluded" (126). The reader might well conclude the same following Johannes Verne's schoolyard fight with Rad Huber in *The Lonesome Gods* (1983).

L'Amour's fictions also sustain and promote another fundamental idea of United States foreign policy—the idea of a racial hierarchy, one which ranks white people—white people from the United States especially—as first, followed by the other races, each assigned certain stereotypical features. Latin Americans were usually thought of as either savage brutes, or Black children, or as lovely *Señoritas* waiting to be rescued (Hunt 60). For many L'Amour readers, since Latin Americans had suffered under the brutality of the Spaniards, and since they had allowed miscegenation, they were an inferior people, not unlike L'Amour's brutal 'greasers' with their ever-present knives, or they were but untutored children, not unlike L'Amour's sun-loving, lazy, easy-going wealthy Californios, or, in more positive terms, like a helpless but lovely woman in need of salvation either from her own barbaric society or from evil foreign designs, reminiscent of the lovely Mariana in *The Californios*, who, when rescued by the strong Anglo American Sean, is being harassed by a crude Mexican suitor.

Such stereotypes were used long prior to the war with Mexico in 1847, although proponents of that war found them especially appropriate as a means to promote their cause.

Once war began, James K. Polk and his expansionist supporters justified their aggressive course by denouncing the enemy in the conventional and contemptuous terms as "ignorant, prejudiced, and perfectly faithless." In this same spirit a New York paper declared, "The Mexicans are *Aboriginal Indians*, and they must share the destiny of their race" (Hunt 60).

Racial stereotypes, such as L'Amour's novels sustain concerning Latin Americans *and* Anglo Americans, were used later to justify United States in its war with Spain. One may note Theodore Roosevelt's "corollary to the Monroe Doctrine [which] asserted the right to force intemperate Latinos to 'obey the primary laws of civilized society'...[in order to] make the regions 'stable, orderly, and prosperous' " (Hunt 132).

More troublesome, perhaps, Louis L'Amour's fictions sustain the myth of the six gun as a weapon for peace. During the last three decades, while the L'Amour Westerns achieved their great popularity, people in the United States, in spite of having to use violence in Viet Nam—not to mention Cuba, the Dominican Republic, Chili, El Salvador, Nicaragua and Panama—have enjoyed great individual prosperity. Perhaps many want to receive the reassuring message of a L'Amour Western, that not only is such violence necessary, but that one simply must learn to live with one's national pistol under one's national pillow in order to maintain the good life. Since World War II the necessity for a strong, assertive, foreign policy has been reinforced over and over again by our leaders as well as by popular culture artifacts such as the novels of Louis L'Amour. We have been taught that maintaining nuclear parity demonstrates our strength, our capability for violence, and therefore keeps the peace. The Louis L'Amour Western provides a supportive analogue for such thought.

Since stories of the United States frontier have such an important place in the psychology and history of the people of the United States, it is not surprising that their development and structure have been given considerable scholarly attention. As noted in the previous chapter, Richard Slotkin's study of the development of the frontier narrative of the United States exemplifies the best of such scholarly attention. Stories of Anglo Americans captured by Native Americans were used by Puritan ministers during the seventeenth century to image for their congregations the moral and physical dangers of venturing too far from the community of believers. Such captivity stories communicated a standard for life on the frontier that soon proved too constrictive for the communities that used such stories as the number of immigrants increased and forced Anglo Americans to intrude further into land held by the race that preceded them. Thus captivity stories soon gave way in popularity to stories of men who had lived in contact with Native Americans, had learned their ways of tracking and killing game in order to survive, yet who had remained loyal to their European cultural and racial background. The story of Daniel Boone, the *Leatherstocking Tales* of James Fenimore Cooper, the stories about Sam Houston and David Crockett, are all about men whose lives announce freedom from European (and Eastern) constrictions upon the individual, yet, paradoxically, demonstrate loyalty to the needs of the people from Europe and the East and recognition of their right to expand, to farm, to build towns, and to 'settle' the land in accordance with their cultural traditions, in spite of the dangers from the race that preceded them and in spite of the dangers from 'White Savages,' those who, unlike the heroes, had allowed contact with Native American to turn them morally and physically into enemies of their own race. The later nineteenth century saw the advent of the 'dime' novel and the introduction of the cowboy hero in place of the tracker and hunter of the earlier idealizations (Smith 90-92). Thus the narrative of the frontier in the United States evolved into the formulaic pattern of the Western.

As Will Wright, in *Six Guns and Society: A Structural Study of the Western,* has demonstrated, the Western, as it evolved, provides an effective means of achieving congruence between opposing needs— historical and psychological—of the people of the United States. The hero's mode of transportation—on horseback—indicates his freedom from more conventional kinds of group transportation, such as wagons, buggies, and, a bit later, trains, even though in countless versions of the Western the lone hero rides in service of those limited to group transportation, such as families, professionals (teachers or doctors whose training has not prepared them to ride alone), or representatives of other kinds of institutionalized civilization. The clothes of the hero tell of his individual strength, of his capacity to survive without the supports of family, town, and government, and yet his buckskins are modest, appropriate for his place, not so unconventional as to make him totally unacceptable to European or Eastern standards. The heroes' wisdom, usually pronounced in pithy statements (a life of frontier action does not permit the effete verbosity of the intellectual) only in form opposes the commonplaces of the dominant culture from which the hero springs. His wisdom is always fixed within the wisdom of his people, modified but a little by the needs of the wilderness world in which he has had to learn to survive.

Other images, while often associated with the appearance or action of the hero, relate to the historical idealization the Western provides, although they do not lose significance in terms of individual modes of conduct. The hero of the Western has lived in the Edenic world of innocence before despoliation by the new people, and thus he has about him an elegiac aura; he is a reminder of a golden past of innocence (Folsom 204). Such associations sanctify the hero and, according to many versions of the story, make him too holy to remain within the society which he precedes. His sainthood requires that he move on to new land still innocent of the intrusion of vulgar civilization. Yet he also represents the violent means necessary to achieve that intrusion. He has had to fight and kill in order to protect the needs of the culture he leads. As such he represents a form of individual behavior not countenanced by the community, for a community is usually intolerant of those who, since they have demonstrated knowledge of the ways of violence, might be prone to use violence again. In either case, as saint and/or scapegoat, the hero must, usually, to purify self and/or the community, move onward to land where, once again it is assumed, the process will be repeated: a prehistorical, mythological innocence and purity will be followed by violence and death as the new race collides with the indigenous, followed by the settling and improvement of the land the new race obtains. As scapegoat, the hero, who carries about him the aura of the violent and 'uncivilized' people who he has helped to displace, is an image of the will of the new people to improve and perfect—to settle—the land. As saint he is an emblem of the Divine Will to move onward. As either he is emblematic of the nation's Manifest Destiny to expand and enable new territory to become part of the new national order. This, then, is the tradition Louis L'Amour's images nurture.

Chapter III
The Latin American Frontier
According to M.L. Estefanía

The name of Louis L'Amour is well known in the United States, even among those who do not read popular fictions about the Old West frontier. He appeared on the covers of national magazines, occasionally on national television, and was billed as the "World's Bestselling Western Writer" (L'Amour, *The Lonesome Gods,* back cover). Yet, in terms of the number of novels written, at the time of his death he may have been far behind a little known (in the United States) Spaniard who also writes Westerns: Marcial Lafuente Estefanía, the real name of a man who in his seventy plus years has written at least 2,203 Westerns. One of his publishers, Editorial Bruguera, S.A. of Barcelona, estimates that two thirds of his titles have had two or three 20,000 copy editions (Ovejero, letter). If 1,500 of his titles have had three editions that would account for 90,000,000 copies in print; if the other 500 have had two editions that would give him at least another 20,000,000 copies. The data comes from 1980, so it is possible that, if Estefanía has not nosed ahead of L'Amour in the race to be the "World's Bestselling Western Writer," he is at least running very close.

Robert Warshow, in *The Immediate Experience,* argues what a variety of scholars and observers have come to believe about the success of such conventionalized fictions—that their success depends upon the degree that their "conventions have imposed themselves upon the general consciousness and become the accepted vehicles of a particular set of attitudes and aesthetic effect" (101). A study of such fictions should explore how they help to shape and reaffirm the "general consciousness" of their audience toward their subject matter—in this case, the frontier experience—and thus how they have helped to shape history. In the broad structural patterns which such fictions share one can discern the way the fictions affirm, and are affirmed by, the history and attitudes of their audience.

At this point some justification of terms used in reference to *audience* seems necessary. The phrase, *Anglo American,* has been used as if one culture, all prevalent and all powerful, guided all Anglo Americans. Obviously, many different ethnic and cultural and linguistic groups live in English dominant parts of the New World. Yet, a certain pattern, which Louis L'Amour's fictions follow, seems to have huge popularity among those varied people. Similarly, the term *Latin American* will be used as if but one pervasive and powerful culture guided the thought and behavior of people living in Latin America. To refer to the diverse cultures and countries of Latin America with just one, all inclusive label might well offend some national sensibilities as well as the truth. Nevertheless, one of Estefanía's publishers, Editorial Bruguera, attests to the distribution of his fictions in Colombia, Argentina, Ecuador, Venezuela, Mexico and, in translation, Brazil (Ovejero, letter). Besides those countries, they are available in Spain, Guatemala, Puerto Rico, the Dominican Republic, as well as on book racks in Denver, Colorado in sections of the city where Spanish is spoken by many people. Such international consumption indicates a considerable degree of consensus among the audience concerning frontier ideology in spite of many differences among nations and races.

Highly conventionalized fictions would not appeal if their audience did not have expectations prior to their experience with the fictional genre. Ones' expectations cannot be satisfied unless one has expectations. The numerous Western films produced in Italy and Spain suggest that those expectations are culture bound, since those films, even though ostensibly set in the Western part of the United States, are clearly different from Westerns produced in the United States. Estefanía's fictions are labeled as Westerns, both by the pictures on their front covers of cowboys locked in deadly shoot outs and the commentary on their back covers. However, an Estefanía fiction is fundamentally different from a typical Western written for an audience in the United States. Of course, a different pattern for thought about frontier life existed in Latin America long before the United States discovered its West and storytellers created the Western. Cultural attitudes toward frontier life existed in Latin America before a truly Western frontier existed in the United States. Consequently, if an author, writing for Hispanic readers, were to completely imitate the pattern of the Anglo American Western, he would have little success since his audience would have different ideas about frontier life. Thus, in spite of the fact that Louis L'Amour's novels have long been available in translation, they are scarcely major items in book stores in Latin America and certainly do not have nearly the distribution and popularity of M.L. Estefanía's novels. Even though the media may have taught Latin American readers that Westerns should be set in the West of the United States in the last century, their culture still instills a very different concept of the frontier than that conveyed by Westerns written for an Anglo audience. Therefore, M.L. Estefanía's fictions are only superficially about life on the United States' frontier and instead conform to prevailing attitudes among Latin American readers concerning frontier life in Latin America.

The frontier in Latin America is conceived of as a brutal place where the weak are devoured by the strong, and where justice must be imposed (and reimposed) through forceful action by representatives of legal and traditional authority from far-off centers of power. Dr. Chanca, the fleet physician who accompanied Columbus on his second voyage in 1493, writing of the very early frontier in Puerto Rico, described the pliant, meek, submissive and good Tainos (the Native Americans who were living in Puerto Rico when the Spaniards arrived) and told how they were set upon continuously by the savage Caribs, who robbed and cannibalized. (The Caribs were Native Americans from the West Indies.) The Spaniard's role, as Dr. Chanca saw it, was simply to protect the interests of the Spanish Crown (Columbus 17-19). Bartolomé de las Casas, who came just a few years after Dr. Chanca, spent most of his life struggling to require that throne to restrain individual Spaniards from abusing Native Americans. Thus, even if the indigenous peoples on the frontiers of Latin America were not always savage and barbaric, the invading Europeans quite often were, just as invading Anglo Americans were often barbaric on the frontiers of North America.

To be sure, Native Americans, evidently from pre-Columbian times, were habitually submissive in Peru and Mexico. The Spaniards had a fairly easy time of it on the frontiers in those countries, once they had subdued the principal leaders of the major civilizations. Nevertheless, "...when it came to less sedentary and cultivated peoples like the Yaquis of the Great Chichimeca and the Araucanians in southern Chile where authoritarian structures were poorly defined, the Spaniards encountered resistance so strong that in some cases it was not until the nineteenth century that the tribes were overcome" (Hamill 18).

The Yaguis and the Araucanian were not the only savages on the frontier in New Spain. During the conquest the conquistadors contributed to the concept of the frontier as a wild and brutal place. According to Octavio Paz, much of the mixing of the races that created the populations in many Latin American countries stems from rape by the conquistadors (65-88).

Unlike the frontier in the United States, as it is commonly conceived, Latin American frontiers are not necessarily located along a fixed—in time and space—line of conquest. Certainly such a line does not exist in Estefanía's fictions, wherein the hero travels from town to town, from West to East, from North to South, discovering conflicts which lead to frontier adventure. However, the Estefanía hero ultimately gains his power to impose order, and indeed has the power to impose order, only within a specific region, such as Kansas, or Texas, or Colorado. Such a pattern concurs with the historical model for *caudillaje*. The *caudillo* gains and maintains his power, among other means, through the use of personal relationships. Family relationships, for example, are stronger in rural areas. Thus the *caudillo* calls on family for support and they respond. Anastasio Somoza of Nicaragua put family in high positions throughout his government. The *compadre* system, by which one achieves a personal relationship with someone by being the godfather of his children, also serves to tie people to a leader. Moreover, the *amigo* relationship is more than that suggested by the word *friend* (Chevalier 44-46). Ultimately, however, such relationships have limitations. One can only be godfather to so many children; one can only have a limited number of relationships. Of course, the *caudillo supremo*, such as Porfirio Diaz, used the strength of local *caudillos*, or *caciques*, to consolidate his own power. He allowed them to make money, but he realized that the central government could have little impact in areas so isolated that they had no contact with that government (Chevalier 49-50). Such a system of *caudillaje* thus leads to regional strong men with ties to a national leader. But the power the individual citizen knows within such a system is the power of the local *caudillo*. Thus the power that imposes order in Estefanía's novels is a regional, not national, power.

Such power, therefore, unlike the power of the Anglo American hero, has spatial limitations. On the Anglo American frontier the fictional hero is usually seen imposing a new order of justice in a place of savagery, either Native American savagery or the savagery of outlaws or of large ranchers who wish to control all of the space. Since the Anglo American frontier hero usually moves onward again after establishing order for the colonists, his role is national rather than regional. He expands national space, rather than maintaining order within a specific region. The hero on Estefanía's frontier often confronts the upstart behavior of men of his own race who have gone beyond their proper social station (in what has been, obviously, a previously established social order.) The Estefanía hero restores a pre-existent, stable and just order, even though, to be sure, that order is only within a specific region of the hinterlands.

To impose such order, in Estefanía's fictional world, requires extreme violence. But, the fictions assume, the order those representatives restore, however much violence may be required for its imposition, is exactly what the people need. The fictions present a heroic image which promises a world purified of evil and disorder. Later in this study we will see how novelists with a more personal vision have used their words to examine the simplistic faith in *caudillaje* Estefanía's fictions sustain.

A discussion of a novelist whose titles numbered 2,203 in 1980 and who, no doubt, has added to that number since that time, must be preceded by a disclaimer: only a sample has been used in this study. Yet the sample demonstrates remarkable predictability. The titles chosen just happened to be available and consisted of about 2%, or forty, fictions from Estefanía's total production. Thirty-one of the 40 are 96 pages long. Most of the earlier fictions—those published in the 1960s—are divided into 90 pages of adventures concerning the life of a single hero followed by a 5 page denouement. Many of the later fictions, published in the 1970s and early 1980s, have two heroes. The first forty-five pages are devoted to the adventures of the lesser hero, the second forty five to those of the slightly greater hero, and the last five to the denouement. The plot frequently involves family, either those who must be protected, such as a sister or an aged parent or grandparent or, occasionally, those who must be fought, such as a father, an uncle, or a cousin from whom the others must be saved. Since the works are extremely predictable, the sample is adequate to demonstrate how Estefanía's fictions promote and sustain the idea of the frontier as a savage place which requires the strength of a *caudillo* to impose order.

One absolutely predictable element in the fictions presents a tempting target for patronizing humor, but then one recalls that what is being presented is compatible with the attitudes of millions of readers. In all the fictions in the sample there is a correlation between the physical stature of a man and his moral and heroic worth—which is to say that in an Estefanía fiction all tall men are heroic and moral. The tallest man is the most heroic and moral. The image of a tall man suggests strength, and in an Estefanía fiction it is from the strength of an individual that the community can obtain peace and stability.

In accord with the savage view of the frontier in Latin America, the villains and the tall heroes are prone to extreme violence. Death, hangings, beatings, floggings, all are common stuff in the pages of Estefanía. Strength must be demonstrated, and it is by means of such violence that the tall heroes demonstrate that they have the necessary hard hand to impose justice by protecting the weak and punishing those who deserve it.

On a more abstract level, the movement in Estefanía's fictions is from the hinterlands to some kind of power center, or, if the action does not move, then it is discovered, in the final pages, that the hero has been sent from or has close (often family) ties to a center of authority. Estefanía is not politically precise. Such centers of authority are frequently of a regional nature, a state capital, for example. As such, in terms of the political traditions in many parts of Latin America, the power in such a center would emanate from *caciques,* or regional political leaders. The power exerted on Estefanía's frontiers is always discovered to be official. Often, in Latin American political tradition, *caudillos* achieve power in the national governments, even if they don't always assume a specific office. Happily, the *caudillos* in Estefanía's fictions seem to have all the official authority necessary to achieve justice.

Action in an Estefanía fiction does not lead to a new form of government or to new people replacing those who have governed prior to the advent of the hero (as, say, prior to the advent of Daniel Boone in Kentucky), but instead the hero goes to the frontier to reaffirm an order which existed prior to the action of a villain. Time moves backwards in the world of Estefanía to a past of order, stability, and justice.

¿*También los cuatreros?* [*Even the Rustlers?*] (1980) offers a good example of the temporal movement in Estefanía. The hero, Ellery, although appearing at first as a simple cowboy, just as an Anglo American conventional Western would have it, returns to his old family ranch to visit his grandfather who, in spite of Ellery's humble appearance, is the wealthiest and most politically powerful rancher in Kansas. The elderly gentleman has ruled benevolently for many years over his vast empire of land and possessions. However, with age and illness, his power has been usurped by unscrupulous members of his own family. Ellery makes short work of his greedy, presumptuous aunts and uncles. Then, with his lifelong friend, Stewart, who is not quite as tall as Ellery, he goes forth to clean up the cattle industry, which the reader discovers to be the fief of Ellery's grandfather. The young heroes find that in Kansas City naive and foolish cowboys have allowed themselves to be lured into boarding a riverboat where card sharks cheat them of their money. Using the influence of his grandfather, Ellery finds an honest judge who, with the help of Ellery and Stewart as enforcers, sees to it that all of the culprits—more or less fifteen—are beaten, shot, and hanged. The riverboat (which had been stolen by the gamblers) is returned to its owner. The naive cowboys are restored to the security of a river front without thieves. Private property and official morality have been reestablished.

The *caudillo* possesses all. He imposes his power through surrogates who are his personal representatives, usually relatives. As Ellery and Stewart continue their inspection of Ellery's grandfather's domain they discover that the packing houses are cheating helpless ranchers. The buyers for the packing houses are dishonest. Ellery's grandfather, luckily, is the major stockholder in the packing house companies, so Ellery and Stewart have full power to rid the companies of the corrupt buyers. But the entire industry is in trouble. The railroad cattle cars are old and often break down. Ellery's grandfather—the reader will not be surprised— is the major stockholder in the company that manufactures cattle cars for the railroad, so the problem is taken care of after a few villains are punished. Finally, the Cattlemen's Association has been taken over by a villain who is preventing the ranchers from getting a fair price for their cattle. Some of the ranchers have resisted, but the leader of the resistance has been put in jail by a corrupt judge. The jailed man's defenseless daughter is saved and the Cattlemen's Association reformed and restored to proper State authority, which, one may safely assume, is closely allied with the authority of Ellery's grandfather.

Ellery and Stewart—with Grandfather in the background—are able to reestablish the cattle industry as a just system for the ranchers and the cowboys. A new system has not been initiated, but rather a continuum of the true order of the past has been assured as members of the *caudillo's* family impose once again the stern but just order the people of the hinterland require. Time has moved backward to a pre-existent order. Within that order the small ranchers and cowboys relate to Ellery's grandfather much as a serf to the lord of the manor, or a tenant farmer in nineteenth century England to the landowner, or a Native American to the *encomendero* during the early years of the frontier in Hispanic America. Within such a system a strong regional leader dominates space— literally possesses all—within a defined area. It does not matter if others own or do not own land within that space: the leader is still the leader. Ellery and Stewart make certain that those who corrupted such a system by usurping position and authority within the family and society are all properly punished.

¿También los cuatreros? was published in 1980. *De Dodge City a Abilene [From Dodge City to Abilene]* was published in 1963. If a significant pattern exists in Estefanía's fictions then that pattern should be apparent in early as well as in later works. The pattern of temporal regression as seen in *¿También los cuatreros?* is closely related to the argument that power emanates from a center of traditional and legal authority, such as the authority of a State government. Such power remains constant; it does not change in time.

Such is the case in *De Dodge City a Abilene.* As the title suggests, the action begins in Dodge City where a relatively tall young man, Lee, has brought cattle from his father's ranch near Abilene, Texas. Lee tries to prove that the gamblers in one of the saloons are taking advantage of the cowboys. He fails, but an even taller young man, Wyoming, enters. Wyoming's name is not without significance; in the final pages the reader discovers that the tall hero is the son of a very important family from the state of Wyoming. He quickly proves that the gamblers are cheating, then shames them, and finally kills them. The frontier, constantly threatened by change, must be controlled and contained by violence.

Impressed by Wyoming's abilities, Lee offers him a job as a cowboy. On their return trip to the ranch of Lee's father they have various adventures with Lee's treacherous relatives in Amarillo, then more problems with treachery in the frontier town of Abilene, but Wyoming kills, beats, maims and/or hangs whoever deserves it. They eventually arrive at the home ranch and Jennifer, Lee's sister, falls in love with Wyoming, and he with her, although he is reluctant to declare himself. Eventually he reveals the reason for his reluctance. Immediately before he met Lee in Dodge City he had been blamed for killing the Sheriff in Cheyenne, the capital of Wyoming, although it was his cousin who committed the crime. The unfortunate, but tall, young man did not betray his cousin but instead left his father's ranch and went on the run. His father, then Governor of Wyoming, was forced to resign due to the scandal.

Nonetheless, Wyoming admits that he loves Jennifer, but before they can marry he must clear his name. He does and his parents learn the truth and come to Abilene to attend the wedding. Since they are indeed people of great wealth (and thus, it is assumed in the fiction, great importance), they are able to give the young couple a $100,000.00 wedding gift. The hero is, after all, scarcely a nobody. He demonstrates his power by demonstrating strength and skill with guns and whips. The plot associates that power with the power of a strong man with extensive possessions as well as ties to the State. It was the great good fortune of the cowboys in Dodge City, and of Lee and his sister, that an extension of such power—the *caudillo's* son, Wyoming—was available to protect them. From such centers of power the weak can find protection. That protection comes to the frontier in the form of a regional strong man, a *caudillo* who knows that orderly life on the frontier demands strength and violence.

¡Es una india! [She's an Indian!] (1981) demonstrates that even those of another race can obtain justice if they have access to the strength, and the violent means of imposing order, available through a *caudillo*. The novel's heroine, a tall blond, the daughter of a Native American man and an Anglo woman his people have captured, scarcely resembles her father. Not surprisingly, it is discovered through the course of the fiction that she is the heiress (through her mother) to the largest ranch in Kansas and that her maternal grandfather is the most important army general in Topeka, the capital of Kansas. Her tall cowboy hero, Ben Strong, turns out to be a highly skilled physician and surgeon and her lifelong, 'oldtimer' friend, "Kansas," a highly respected lawyer. The heroine gains the respect and admiration of all the decent and responsible people in Topeka. Thus, being of mixed parentage does not prove at all damaging to one's looks or prospects if, by chance, one is born without any of the characteristics of the less dominant race and has blood ties with the *caudillo* (her grandfather) of the region.

La leyenda de un fraile [The Legend of a Monk] (1963) illustrates Estefanía's theme of justice as the child of power while depicting a racial hierarchy on the frontier. Rufus, a Negro blacksmith, too old to do hard work in his shop, is counseled by Elinore, the fair heroine, to hire a young Mexican, Jorge, who comes from an impoverished family. Rufus does, and Jorge expresses his gratitude to Elinore. Later, due to evil machinations, Jorge and Rufus are arrested. Jorge's pretty young wife goes to visit her husband in jail, where she is taunted by the corrupt jailers, then thrown to the floor and nearly raped. Happily, Bill, who is quite tall, saves her, disarms and hangs the four jailers, then frees Jorge and Rufus. Bill, it might be noted, is not only quite tall but also the son of a very important family from Dallas. The responsibility of the stronger races, demonstrated by the just action of the tall son of a *caudillo,* is to protect those who are unable to protect themselves.

However, *El final del indio Apache [The End of the Apache Indian]* (1980) also treats racial relations, but illustrates that the strong man on the frontier must be ready to use violence to control the indigenous who rebel against established authority. The hero (tall) has grown up among Native Americans and has acquired their skills. But unlike Natty Bumppo, of James Fenimore Cooper's *Leatherstocking Tales,* Estefanía's hero has not developed an appreciation for the good qualities of those who taught him how to survive in the wilderness. He hates the entire race. He works for the army. Eventually the army must capture Puma, the hero's Native American brother by adoption who, in spite of having been given an Anglo education, rebels. While the hero distracts Akima, the man who adopted him and served as his father, by talking with him inside a tepee, the soldiers hang all of Akima's people, the tall hero's childhood friends, with the exception of Puma, Akima's birth son. When Akima and the hero leave the tepee they are confronted by rows of hanging human bodies. The hero, of course, is not surprised nor emotionally moved, since he has planned the entire operation. The old man, Akima, goes peacefully along to the fort, even though he is allowed to refer to the hero as ungrateful, which seems a bit of an understatement. At the fort it is disclosed that Puma has been spared only that he may be publicly hanged. The hero speaks with the old man who raised him and determines that the shock of all the events has made him too crazy and dangerous to be allowed to live. So both Akima and Puma are hanged so that they might serve as examples for other rebel Native American leaders.

During the conquest of Mexico, Sepúlveda and Cortés, among many others, advocated and practiced the use of violent methods to subdue the rebellious on the frontiers. Such methods would seem to still have a sympathetic audience among Estefanía's readers.

As Eric R. Wolf and Edward C. Hansen have observed in *The Human Condition in Latin America,* the hierarchical structure of Hispanic society reinforces the centralist concept of government which the *caudillo* epitomizes. Within the family the analogue for such a structure is the power of the father. In *Sangre junto al río [Blood Along the River]* (1963) Estefanía offers his readers a fantasy of revolution wherein the most immediate representative of hierarchy, the father, is proven culpable, deposed, and finally true order reestablished with the help of the government.

The father steals cattle from a widow and land which—through maternal inheritance—properly belongs to his son. The son, the tall hero, happily has the official support of the Texas Rangers. However, the son's rebellion against his father leads to violence as abstract and impersonal as pornographic sex; there is indeed a quantity of blood along the river. On pages 59 and 60 the hero and his pal (an undercover Ranger) kill thirteen men. From pages 64 through 66 four more are killed as a crooked lawyer and three of his hired guns are beaten and dragged behind horses. Bad men are forced to their knees to have their teeth kicked out. An unconscious man—beaten unconscious by a Ranger—deserves more, the hero feels, and so he continues to beat him until the man is dead. Fourteen men are killed in a shoot-out at the ranch. The rangers pistol whip the hero's father to death. Joan, the rustler's woman, is shot, and so the story goes.

Yet, while the hierarchy of the family can be successfully challenged by State power, Estefanía' readers do not want to question the male dominated family structure. In fact, it is the responsibility, even the moral duty, of a man to punish his wife should she act contrary to social norms. In *¡Es una india! [She's an Indian!]* (1980), Estefanía's fiction demonstrates how the strong male in the family provides an analogue for the strong man in larger social structures. In the fiction the wife of the kind judge (who has helped the well-connected, wealthy but mixed-breed heroine) gossips about the heroine's mixed blood. She tells army officials that the girl is a half-breed, thinking this will cause them to place the young woman on a reservation. The judge is infuriated with his wife. He beats her and then throws her out of his house. The army major who comes to investigate is so angered with the old gossip that he also beats her. The heroine, upon hearing what the judge's wife has said about her, ropes the woman and drags her through the streets behind a horse. Finally, while the injured woman is being treated by the doctor, she manages, quite unfortunately, to mumble a few more deprecatory words about the heroine. The doctor then beats her and throws her into the street. The initial beating administered by her husband, reiterated by various members of the community, would seem to have public support. As the *caudillo* must use violent force to impose his order on society as a whole, so the husband must use violent force to impose his order within the family. The image of a strong, dominant male recalls for readers an entire structure of relationships as well as ideals for behavior.

As may be seen, Estefanía's *caudillos* enforce conservative moral and behavioral standards. One should not gamble with gamblers. One should not cheat. One should not steal. The virtues celebrated are abstract: honor, courage, courtesy, and honesty. The vices denounced are but the other sides of the same coins: honor becomes perverted vengeance, courage becomes bravado, courtesy becomes harassment of the weak, and honesty becomes the trickery of card sharks and rustlers. Such virtues and vices are timeless, and thus the romance fictions depict a static, unchanging world order, one in which it is best for the individual to accept his lot rather than to attempt to improve it. Should one make such an attempt he or she is likely to violate rigid social and moral rules and be punished by the authority of the *caudillo*. The violent form of that punishment attests to the rigid faith the audience must have in the rules. Yet, subconsciously, the brutality in the novels must also allow the readers a sense of release from the rules, a wild and self-righteous orgy of release, all in the name of justice and morality.

As has been noted elsewhere in this study, the hero of the Anglo American frontier fiction lives and derives his strength from knowledge acquired in the hinterlands of space. He thus contributes to an explosive frontier, one which is ever expanding as the hero, having helped the colonists to establish an Anglo American settlement, moves onward to help impose that civilization in other places. In contrast, Estefanía's frontier is implosive. The heroes in an Estefanía fiction derive their strength from contacts with centers where strong men—*caudillos*—govern with benevolent—if sometimes violent—power. Estefanía's reader evidently accepts the idea that civilizing power stems from population and political centers. The movement in an Estefanía fiction is inward from the hinterlands to the capitals of states, and from the hinterlands of individuality to established social and political authority—embodied, ironically, in a single individual.

Caudillaje has international, as well as national, political implications. On the early frontiers in Latin America the center of authority and power was Madrid. Soon after independence from Spain was won by Latin America, in the early part of the nineteenth century, a vast surplus of capital in England led to investment in Latin America. Many *caudillos* who were heads of nations found they could get British loans easier than taxing or borrowing from their own people (Bunge 128-129). "Toward the end of the century the exploitation of new sources of mineral and agricultural wealth, together with a strong influx of foreign investments, gave caudillos more dependable leverage for control." . . . "[F]inancial resources and the protective favor of foreigners allowed the leader to govern by remote control. . . . Such men were Venezuela's Guzman Blanco, Mexico's Porfirio Diaz, [and] Guatemala's Barrios" (Morse 63). Such *caudillos* invited foreign businessmen to invest heavily in Latin America.

When United States investors joined British investors they built, among other things, railroads. Mexico's railroad system illustrates the way foreign capital investment led to an infrastructure that lends itself to continued foreign domination. Since United States and British investors were interested in access to the raw materials from Mexico, railroad lines were built from the center of the country to connections with major lines in the United States, or from the center to port cities where products could be sent by water to international markets. The network only casually serves to link the country together; it primarily serves to enable the country to be exploited.

Just as the *caudillos* learned that it was easier to get foreign capital than it was to extract capital from their own people, so the foreign investors learned that it was better to deal with a *caudillo* than it was to work with a troublesome democracy. As foreign capital, mostly from the United States, took over, "Large private companies, most of them foreign, which exploit or sell oil, tropical fruits, sugar, and other export products, [became]...proprietors of large enterprises and huge estates with enormous incomes. Naturally they...feared the demands of their employees, the requests for land from the peasants, the nationalistic and xenophobic tendencies of the mob, and they...also feared popular troubles which might compromise the success of their businesses. Thus their representatives have sometimes shown certain preferences for authoritarian government which seemed to them more capable of insuring order and better disposed to support their interests in exchange for financial and even political support" (Chevalier 50). Given such economic and political realities, Latin American *caudillos* must perforce be subservient to the financial center of their world—the United States.

Now, after nearly a century of a form of colonial status with the United States, there is a tired, bitter joke that says when the United States catches a cold, Latin America sneezes. The joke acknowledges political reality in the New World: the center of power is not local or national government, whether democratic or military, leftist or right wing, but rather the United States, the 'colossus of the North,' as it is often referred to in the southern part of the New World. One highly visible print and electronic image of the United States is that presented by the Western. The conventions of Estefanía's Westerns, written for a Latin American audience, celebrate the strong man who can bring peace—using violence—to the frontier. Estefanía adapts the genre to the theme of the strong man as the means by which a strong government, dominated by a *caudillo,* can bring order and justice to the frontier. His version is obviously well received by many millions of readers in Latin America. Estefanía readers respect strength and expect their leaders to use it wisely for the greater good of all. Nurtured by Estefanía's many millions of fictions, the system of *caudillaje* sinks its roots ever deeper in Latin America.

Perhaps worse yet, through the fictions of Estefanía, many Latin American readers learn to look to a heroic type identified with the United States, the cowboy, to fulfill the role of the *caudillo.* The lessons of economic and political reality are reinforced by the fictions many read, as they learn, through those fictions, to look to the United States for the leadership and control provided by the *caudillo* within their own cultural tradition. The tall heroes in an Estefanía fiction are almost all blond. They *are* centers of power. Since the real center of power is now the United States, the structure of Estefanía's fictions insinuate that heroes from the United States can bring peace and stability. Thus the content of Estefanía's fictions insinuate a form of psychological dependence. The area's political and economic reality has a symbiotic relationship with one of its dominant fictions.

Chapter IV
Gene Autry's Song Filled Travels in Latin America

The Western Musical and the World

Fans of M.L. Estefanía may well make large claims for the popularity of the bard of their special explanation of the frontier. Estefanía knows, however, that the United States frontier has a peculiar kind of world wide romantic appeal, and therefore, rather than writing stories about the struggle between descendants of the Spaniards and Peruvian Native Americans, or between Spanish or Creole pioneers and the Miskitos in Nicaragua, he tells stories about cowboys and Native Americans in Wyoming, Colorado, Arizona and Kansas. He knows that images drawn from films about the United States frontier have special entertainment value. His special skill is his ability to recall those images in narratives that are in accord with Latin American frontier ideology.

Images of the West of the United States in the nineteenth century have had a remarkable relationship with the entertainment industry in the last one hundred years. For that matter, the United States frontier had an important place in the entertainment business prior to the twentieth century. James Fenimore Cooper's *Leatherstocking Tales,* as well as other, earlier, versions of the United States' frontier story, created frontier images that recalled, to readers familiar with the values of their culture, ideals for domestic behavior and international expansion.

However, late in the nineteenth century, certain developments gave the story even greater power. It was at that time that Ned Buntline, a writer for *The New York Weekly,* discovered, in the Hollywood sense of the word, William Cody (Smith 104). Cody was working as a scout and hunter for the Army. Since Cody had a reputation as a buffalo hunter, and since Buntline wanted to package him for the eastern reading public, he called Cody *Buffalo Bill* in the stories he wrote for his newspaper. William Cody, no fool, adopted the persona Buntline created and galloped hell bent for leather into show business on his own. He created his own show, seen live, a traveling pageant, circus, spectacle, and historical representation of the frontier wars between colonists and Native Americans. It played well in America and in Europe, perhaps because Buffalo Bill clearly understood the function of the hero as the predecessor to colonization in the frontier story. He, of course, acted the role of the hero, and in his later years, with perhaps just a touch of confused romanticism, proclaimed, "I stood between savagery and civilization most all of my early days" (Smith 107).

Buffalo Bill was a version of the trapper-hunter as hero of the frontier fiction of the United States. By the late decades of the nineteenth century, trappers and hunters were out of date. Native Americans were mostly defeated or being subjected to pacification programs; the country was mapped and quickly becoming colonized; a man in buckskins was an anachronism when ready-made clothes were available to almost everyone. A new kind of hero was needed. In the 1880s drovers, men who made their living tending other men's livestock on the prairies of North America, became the romantic replacement for the trapper-hunter as hero. The cowboy, as hero, was invented during the late decades of the nineteenth century (Smith 109). Ironically, the first use of the term cited in the *Oxford English Dictionary* refers to *cow-boys* as British partisans during the revolutionary war "who were exceedingly barbarous in the treatment of their opponents who favored the American cause." The first citation to the word in its current sense is dated 1882. The dictionary's examples include citations from an 1884 June edition of the *Miles City Press* (Montana) and the September 10, 1887 edition of the *Spectator*. The *cow-boy*, the *OED* tells us, "...does his work on horseback, and leads a rough life, which tends to make him rough and wild in character (1112)."

In that same year, 1887, Prentice Ingraham, with what evidently was an acute or lucky sense for popular taste, saw that the often shabby and poorly paid drover could, with his new name—*cowboy*—become a suitable replacement for the trapper-hunter as the frontier hero for the United States. Using Buck Taylor, a performer with Buffalo Bill's traveling show as a model, Ingraham created the first fictional cowboy hero (Smith 110).

Thus a symbiotic relationship developed between the demands for entertainment and the historical existence of certain frontiersmen such as Boone, Cody and a variety of gunmen and just plain cowboys whose stories lent themselves to idealizations, and thus for the communication of frontier ideology.

The relationship was technically consummated by the invention of moving pictures. In 1887—that same momentous year the cowboy hero was born—Thomas Alva Edison employed a young Englishman, William Kennedy Dickson, to experiment with methods for providing visual images to go along with Edison's phonograph—in short, to use the technology of photography to create moving pictures with sound (Ramsaye 55).

Conceived in the same year, the cowboy and the moving picture were made for each other. In 1889 George Eastman developed flexible celluloid film and the movies were on their way (Ramsaye 62). In 1894,

Buffalo Bill, Annie Oakley, and a special feature, a Sioux tribal dance, hit the screen (Ramsaye 83). To be sure, the film was only fifty feet long, so the audience didn't dare blink unless they wanted to watch it a second time. Entrepreneurs made other short documentaries of the West, depicting a cattle round-up or buffalo grazing on the plains, and sometimes brief depictions more in accord with the 'savage' image of the West, such as stagecoach holdups or Native Americans scalping their victims (Everson 14). While dime novel cowboys were being established as the standard frontier heroes in print, modifications in film technology enabled longer pictures to be produced. In 1903, when the cowboy hero and the motion pictures were just sixteen years old, the first Western film—with a plot and characters and setting—was made (Everson 14). Although filmed near Paterson, New Jersey, with a hero who couldn't stay on his horse, "The Great Train Robbery" was, nonetheless, a Western (Horowitz 55). It was a huge success, so it was quickly followed by a sequel, "The Great Bank Robbery" of 1904 (Ramsaye 419). G.M. Anderson, a former vaudeville performer, played Bronco Billy, the first film cowboy hero. He made hundreds of one and two reel Westerns.

As Bronco Billy's popularity boomed, D.W. Griffith, Thomas H. Ince and others made Westerns which celebrated the survival skills of the cowboy, lamented the inevitable passing of the Native American from his Edenic world, or quite contrarily, condemned Native Americans for their savagery. The Western and the entertainment industry continued their close partnership arrangement. Thomas H. Ince made a deal with "the entire Miller Brothers' 101 Ranch Wild West Show, a company with a huge entourage of cowboys, horses, wagons, buffaloes, and other accessories." With this equipment, he filmed a two-reel spectacle in 1911 entitled "War on the Plains"...(Fenin and Everson 67). William S. Hart, whose credentials as a cowboy included stage experience as a Shakespearian actor, found new professional life on the cinematic frontier in films such as "On the Night Stage" (1914), "Hell's Hinges" (1916), "Wild Bill Hickok" (1923), and "Tumbleweed" (1924).

To be sure, men and women still worked with cattle on Western prairies, as they had for many years before the cowboy's entertainment value was discovered. Horses were still gentled for daily use, corrals were still built, and cattle were still gathered and driven to far away markets. Nevertheless, the 'cowboy' and entertainment, in the public mind, were tightly linked. Not all entertainment involved cowboys, but for the ever increasing number of Americans who were leaving their agrarian past and moving to towns and cities, the cowboy was associated with entertainment, not work. No doubt, for many, the distinction between the 'reality' of the cowboy working on the plains, representing the American ideals of rugged individualism and hard work as the road to survival and prosperity, and the 'reality' of the cowboy as a survivalist, like those survivalists who had prepared the way for Anglo colonization in the west, as well as the 'reality' of the star on stage or screen, a 'star' with that special kind of mystique that becomes reality for those who want to be entertained, became blurred. The image of the cowboy star came to evoke a mélange of American ideals. The image was seldom examined by the public. Like most images, it provided a convenient shortcut for rational thought.

Probably all of the 'realities' of the image of the cowboy were accepted by many people without question. Soon, certain images, such as rope and costume, used on stage, were enough to suggest the totality of the Western frontier experience. Since the story of the survivor on the frontier was well known, cowboys as entertainers, in pageants, on stage or in films, needed very few images from the basic frontier story in order to recall the whole of the story. Repetition, as Umberto Eco has argued, forms the basis for escapist play, and the frequent repetition of the play pattern of the Western had made it familiar to audiences and readers. Thus, for the sake of entertainment, the totality of the narrative was redundant even in the early years of the Western. Nevertheless, the cowboy as entertainer accrued extra added attractions, perhaps because more and more of the audience began to perceive the cowboy's life as part of the world of play and the added attractions emphasized the play aspect of the performance. Audiences demanded less of the cowboy and more of the entertainer.

In the mid 1920s, with the development of the slick, *streamlined* Western, Hoot Gibson and Ken Maynard—both primarily performers— became popular using numerous show business rodeo stunts (Fenin and Everson 149). Such 'cowboys' were more closely tied to the unreal world of entertainment. In real life, William S. Hart's friends "...included Western lawmen Wyatt Earp, 'Uncle Billy' Tilghman, and 'Bat' Masterson, as well as Will Rogers, artists Charles Russell and James Montgomery Flagg, and even Pat O'Malley, a reformed outlaw who had ridden with the Al Jennings gang" (Fenin and Everson 104). Hart, an actor and entertainer, evidently liked to live close to the 'reality' of the cowboy, the lawman, and the outlaw, the material from which the unreal world of his films was concocted. Tom Mix appeared with the Miller Brothers' 101 Ranch Wild West Show, clearly a member of the entertainment world. After his time with the Wild West Show he was Sheriff in Oklahoma and Kansas—doing, in truth, what entertainment cowboys did in the dime novels and Western films (Fenin and Everson 110). Later, Mix drifted into Mexico, joined Madero, and at one point was in front of a firing squad, acting out, in reality, the kind of international adventure Westerns often depicted (Fenin and Everson 111). His life must have further confused the dual—entertainment and reality— function of the cowboy in the public mind.

The combination of the film and the Western—so real and yet so artificial—was the perfect medium for advocating the U.S. frontiersman as an image of a virtuous and trustworthy hero, one who could be counted upon to bring moral order to savage frontiers. Trade papers carried announcements declaring: "William S. Hart pictures are always inspiring—they make folks breathe deeper" or, in publicizing "The Narrow Trail" "Better a painted pony than a painted woman" (Fenin and Everson 128). Hart frequently played the good-bad man who "occasionally got roaring drunk...and forced the heroine into marriage with him at gun point." But such "...ungentlemanly behavior always took place at the beginning of the film...allowing Hart ample time for remorse and self-sacrifice, and allowing the heroine equally ample time to fall genuinely in love with him and present him with a child" (Everson 41).

The standards for proper behavior suggested by the image of the cowboy were used to judge the behavior of others, women, or, as shall be seen, people from other countries or other cultures. Tom Mix's conception of the kind of Western he made illustrates the idealism inherent in the Western, an idealism that carries with it the notion that it is appropriate for the moral man to interfere with whatever he finds not to his liking. As Mix put it, "I ride into a place owning my own horse, saddle, and bridle. It isn't my quarrel, but I get into trouble doing the right thing for somebody else. When it's all ironed out, I never get any money reward. I may be made foreman of the ranch and I get the girl, but there is never a fervid love scene" (Fenin and Everson 117). The cowboy provided an idealized image for the audience against which the behavior of others could be judged.

Such idealism, of course, defies time, but the Western had a peculiar capacity to promote timeless ideals while admitting evidence of change. In Westerns men ride horses in order to catch trains, automobiles, and even airplanes, and some characters, usually the heroes, dress like cowboys (with decorative fringe and glitter added for entertainment value) while others, often the villains, dress in contemporary clothing. Anachronisms in Western film and comic books sustain the old standards, for the images therein suggest frontier values sufficiently to enable the viewers to judge new behavior against those values. As Fenin and Everson observe, "It was, of course, in the Western that the old values were primarily reflected, in a cinematic sense, and in a real sense for America, too;..."(43). Perhaps those values seemed even more precious to the audience as people were required to adapt to new technology and historical change.

To be sure, anachronisms developed quite naturally in the Western. When Westerns were first filmed, the 'history' being presented was nearly contemporary. California was ranch country, so the time and place of Westerns was very close to the time and place of the actual making of the films. Entertainment and reality were almost at one with each other. In the early part of the twentieth century, when filming began in California, the state had been incorporated as part of the nation for little more than a half century. Many very real cowboys from the days of ranching in California found work helping to make films to entertain the rest of the nation.

For that matter, trains, emblems of technological change in Westerns, might not be considered anachronistic. Trains were important in the historical opening of the West and are prominent as conventional elements of the Western. Yet while more and more technological developments were used, the horse and the cowboy prevailed as the preferred method of transportation, just as the old values of the frontier prevailed in the Western.

The use of frontier values to judge new technological and historical experience enabled the Western to travel—in fact, invited the Western to travel—to distant places where frontier values could be used to judge and correct behavior that violated those values. William S. Hart, for example, "was very fond of the plot of the Westerner coming east, overcoming the smooth chicanery of city crooks by using common sense and Western brawn, and then returning home" (Fenin and Everson 80). Tom Mix traveled the Western screen to exotic places such as Arabia and Ruritania. "Tom Mix in Arabia" was made by Mix for Fox, and Mix's "Rough Riding Romance" had a Ruritanian background, as did "My Pal, the King" (Fenin and Everson 117).

Meanwhile, as the film/Western twins were growing up, back at the ranch many changes were made. Townships were laid out, property surveyed, deeds registered, and along with all that, schools, churches, stores, restaurants, hotels, social clubs and service societies established. Indeed, in 1893, Frederick Jackson Turner, in the same paper in which he defined the frontier in the United States, noted the end of the frontier epoch in the history of the United States (Turner 37). The frontier, Turner argued, had promised an endless horizon for expansion and development, and that promise had a great effect on the way people thought and behaved. However, the horizon, by the late nineteenth century, had been reached. The continental United States had been colonized. According to the United States census, which Turner cites, there was no longer a frontier within the United States.

It is, however, one thing to fill geographical space and quite another thing to make people think differently about fundamental matters—such as nation building, expansion, and the proper way a government should govern—when the stories the people read and see and hear continue to provide the same images for thought as that which existed before the space was filled. A geographical limit had, after all, been reached before when the need for territorial expansion had led to the war with

Mexico in 1846. Perhaps it was inevitable that, once such a limit was reached for the second time, Latin America should again become the obvious area for expansion.

Early films reflected—or guided—thought concerning Latin America as an appropriate frontier for expansion. Simply a recitation of a few of the titles suggests the way frontier thought was the subject matter of films depicting relations with Latin countries, especially, of course, with Mexico. "California," (MGM) depicted the "conflict between the United States and Mexico in 1845..., after which California was added to the Union" (Fenin and Everson 158-159). George Fitzmaurice directed "Rose of the Golden West," which featured Gilbert Roland and Mary Astor as loyal Californians, and Gustav Von Seyffertitz as the villain. The film treated "the old situation of California under the Mexican flag, almost becoming Russian territory,"...(Fenin and Everson 172). Some of the many films depicting the 1836 war between Mexico and Texas were: "The Martyrs of the Alamo," "Man of Conquest," "The Last Command," "The Man from the Alamo," "The First Texan," and "The Alamo." "Man of Conquest" (1939) "dealt with the political and military career of Sam Houston (Richard Dix) culminating in the Texans' war of independence against the Mexicans, and the battles of the Alamo and San Jacinto" (Fenin and Everson 123, 129).

Such films nourished basic ideas about the policy of the United States toward Latin America. In the last decades of the nineteenth century the cowboy became the national image for an expansionist frontier ideology as "the old vision of greatness and liberty regained its hold on policy" (Hunt 36). Although many intellectuals opposed the idea, on the grounds that national expansion would limit liberty at home, the idea of foreign expansion, and thereby national greatness, unified the country and became an accepted verity during the 1890s (Hunt 19-45). Popular evangelist Josiah Strong published *Our Country* in 1885, in which he promised his countrymen that God was "preparing mankind to receive our impress" (Strong 178). Strong was convinced that, as successor to the British and beneficiaries of the westward movement of civilization, Americans would turn commerce, missionary work, and colonization toward shaping "the destinies of mankind" (Hunt 37). Through film the cowboy image was soon to achieve far more widespread distribution than the frontier story had ever had before and thereby further reinforce the idea of an expansionist foreign policy with the American public.

At this time, with public sentiment aroused by newspaper stories of Spanish atrocities in Cuba, and given the prevalent ideas of the inferiority of Latin American people who needed salvation and training for democracy, President McKinley claimed that control of the Philippines, Cuba, and Puerto Rico was a "great trust" which the nation carried "under the providence of God and in the name of human progress and civilization" (Hunt 38). However, whatever the nation, encouraged by film and print narrative, may have imagined concerning its manifest destiny, such direct methods for expansion could not be justified. Latin American nations were recognized as legitimate; they were scarcely comparable to Native American nations which were so non-European.

Still, new forms for expansion were needed, since "Recurrent economic crises—first in the 1870s, again in the 1880s, and finally most severely in the 1890s—made foreign markets seem, at least to some, indispensable to the nation's future prosperity" (Hunt 37). Commercial interests led the way. Hollywood represented one such commercial interest. The frontier vision that had inspired expansionist nation building policies provided a convenient justification for commercial expansion into Latin America. Westerns were sent from Hollywood to the rest of the hemisphere. Latin Americans soon saw their film screens filled with stalwart blond cowboy heroes establishing proper order on the frontier by giving colonists the right to settle on land free from the fear of Native American savagery—or by giving colonists the right to build their homes free from the fear of old fashioned ranch owners who behaved like feudal lords, defying progress and civilized order.

In the early 1920s Hollywood was making 500 to 700 films per year. On the other hand, the Latin American film industry lagged behind. By means of aggressive marketing, Hollywood products dominated hemispheric screens (Mora 22). Western films prepared the way, both in the United States and in Latin American, for expansion by providing images which taught patterns for Anglo frontier relations with Latin America.

The Western film established a racial hierarchy between Anglo Americans and Latin Americans by first imaging a general racial hierarchy. Native Americans were shown to be either savages or weak and in need of the protection of Anglo heroes. "The Vanishing American," based on a novel by Zane Grey, begins by establishing the story of the cliff dwellers who, "because of the sense of security that had come to them from living in caves on the inaccessible sides of cliffs, became lazy...[until] a more sturdy and warlike race descended upon and exterminated them" (Fenin and Everson 169). It goes on to tell the story of contemporary Native Americans, who fought well in World War I but returned to their reservation to find that the government agent was a drunk and a cheat. They put their faith in an Anglo schoolteacher (Lois Wilson) but she is off in Washington while the agent takes away their land and homes and forces their women and children to live in the desert. As the Native Americans are about to attack the Anglo Americans, Naphaie (the son of a chief and a young native American leader), tells them that the schoolteacher has returned and that the wicked government agent has been fired from his position. The Native Americans revolt anyway and the former agent is killed by an arrow while Naphaie is killed by a stray bullet. "Bidding his people to obey the government, he [Naphaie] dies, the brave son of a disappearing race" (Fenin and Everson 169). The parallel racial destiny of the cliff dwellers and contemporary Native Americans justifies Anglo confiscation of land. Had the Native Americans remained battle ready they would never have lost their land to the new race, the Anglo Americans who defeated them.

The image of the Native Americans, weak and dependent, presumes that Anglo dominance was not only natural but inevitable. "Braveheart" (1926) argues that the Native Americans needed to adopt the culture that had dominated them. The film stars Rod La Rodque as a "college-educated, football-playing Indian who returns to lead his people in the ways of the white man" (Fenin and Everson 171). "Broken Arrow" (1950) was the first film in years to present Native Americans "as sympathetic human beings with a genuine grievance...." Nevertheless, true to a basic tenet of United States frontier ideology, Native Americans were not quite human enough to marry, for Debra Paget, the beauty about to marry James Stewart, the frontiersman, is killed just before the end (Fenin and Everson 281). "Prior to 'Broken Arrow,' " according to Fenin and Everson's study, "there had been no concerted effort to present the Indian sympathetically since the early days of Ince and films like 'The Heart of an Indian' ".... True, the Indian was not always presented as a hostile savage, but even when he was shown sympathetically, he was merely portrayed as a childlike native" (282).

The Westerns imaged Hispanics as either villains, usually with knives, or weak and in need of the protection of Anglo heroes. "In 'The Taking of Luke McVane' Hart [William S.] played a gambler who falls in love with a saloon dancer after protecting her from the unwanted advances of drunken Mexicans" (Fenin and Everson 79). In "Hell's Hinges" one of the subtitles which introduces the villain, Silk Miller, tells us the following: "Mingling the oily craftiness of a Mexican with the deadly treachery of a rattler, no man's open enemy, and no man's friend" (Fenin and Everson 86).

Either as savages or as children untutored in the ways of progress and civilization, Native Americans scarcely had the right to space Anglo Americans considered open for colonization. In the same pattern, because they were presented as either villains or as weak and in need of Anglo protection, Latin Americans were not considered 'real' owners of land, even if they had occupied it for centuries. The preeminent position of the United States in the entertainment industry, coupled with the close ties between the Western and the entertainment industry, enabled the Western to confirm a pattern for the historical relationship between Anglo and Latin Americans in the Americas, a pattern based in racism expressed early in the history of the nation by James K. Polk who, during the war for control of Texas called the Mexicans "ignorant, prejudiced, and perfectly faithless," a people very like Native Americans and who, therefore, according to a New York paper, would and should share the fate of the Native Americans (Hunt 60). The Western became a powerful persuader concerning frontier relations between Anglo and Latin America. It maintained the existent ideological basis for an expansionist United States frontier policy in Latin America while promoting dependency among certain groups within the Latin American mass audiences upon the United States for the resolution of internal problems.

Gene Autry's Musical Westerns, one part Western and two parts entertainment, illustrate such generalizations. Following the tradition of their film genre, the highly conventionalized, formulaic, Gene Autry musical Westerns link the worlds of entertainment and the cowboy. To many, with rather simple, representational views of the Western, a musical Western seems like a terrible aberration. They are certain that drovers working on the prairie seldom broke into song—at least song backed by the resonant harmony of the Cass County Boys (who often appeared in Gene Autry Films) and a full orchestra (which often accompanied Gene Autry as he sang). In fact, a musical Western is but the natural result of one major tendency that prevailed throughout the evolution of the Western—the blending of entertainment with an idealized view of the history of the expansion of the United States.

Like many cowboy stars before him, Gene Autry had an entertainment background. Born in Tioga, Texas, he sang as a boy in the church choir. When a young man he worked as a telegraph operator in Chelsea, Oklahoma. Soon he began singing in Chelsea restaurants, carnival shows, and on the Chelsea radio station. Evidently people liked his pleasant voice. One evening Will Rogers, who had ties in Oklahoma, came into the telegraph office and heard him sing. Later, perhaps at Will Roger's instigation, Autry signed a contract with Columbia Records. He soon appeared as a regular on NBC's "National Barn Dance" radio program and then moved to films, his first role a minor one in the film, "In Old Santa Fe," released in 1934 starring Ken Maynard. It was appropriate that his first film should have a Latin American flavor since many of his later films were to capitalize on that aspect of the Western.

It was also appropriate, given the pattern for his films in the future, that his first starring role should be in a serial filled with anachronisms and a heavy mixture of action and show business entertainment (Miller 87-92). "The Phantom Empire" (1935), portrays the adventures of a singing cowboy who discovers an underground city called Murania and who must rush back and forth from adventures in Murania to be in time to sing on his radio show.

Autry's Westerns continued the tradition of idealism inherent in the genre. His character "never shot an adversary first, never hit one first, never hit a man smaller than he was, never smoked or took a drink of beer or booze" (Miller 92). If, occasionally, he demonstrated an interest in a girl, he did so in the most restrained puritanical fashion. Frequently his character could be misunderstood by society, or perhaps tricked by a villain, and as a result he might find himself momentarily on the wrong side of the law in a world that seemed to have forgotten the traditional values of the Western, but invariably that remnant from the savage tradition—wherein a few, like William S. Hart, had actually been disposed to unsavory actions—of the Western was quickly banished as Autry proved himself the kind of man who could be trusted to set things in order on the frontier.

Gene Autry's films were full of anachronisms; on his great horse, Champion, he chased, and caught, automobiles, trucks, and airplanes, which were usually used by villains who thought they could escape judgment according to Gene's Western values. Gene Autry's costume, while never as outrageous as those used in some films by his competitor, Roy Rogers, smacked usually of the world of entertainment rather than the everyday world of the drover. Autry's role frequently had some kind of connection with the entertainment industry; for example, he often played a rodeo performer (usually down on his luck) or a singing cowboy for a radio program. However, his films usually used character, plot, or setting elements in order to establish Autry as a man of the people, a normal and representational cowboy, who just happened to have a knack for singing. Because the myth of the West and the entertainment world were so intertwined there was a need for verification. Without some sense, among the audience, that the character Autry played was that of a 'real' cowboy, and not *just* an entertainer, there could be little possibility for melodramatic action which was essential to the cowboy game being played. Moreover, the fundamental, agrarian and nationalistic truths, which the audience associated with the West, demanded authentication if the Western film were to satisfy the needs of its clients.

Such could be achieved rhetorically by establishing the 'real' West as the domain of the star, Gene Autry, and contrasting that with Eastern, Hollywood, or foreign characters of obvious inferior capacities, and especially inferior capacities as cowboys. Gene Autry, as a representative of the old values of the frontier, could therefore judge the flippant and superficial new fashioned career woman or the gangsters from the East or anyone unfamiliar with the ways of the West—on occasion, an entire foreign culture.

The device served to enable Gene Autry's moral judgment—at one with the heart of the West—to prevail in all situations. In short, Gene Autry's films used conventional elements of the Western which had been developed long before he reached the screen. The emphasis on musical entertainment in his films stressed one aspect of the tradition—perhaps at the expense of the other, representational, aspect—but that made those films nonetheless a part of the tradition of the Western. Not surprisingly, like many other films that made up that tradition, they promoted the idea that the job of the frontiersman, in this case the cowboy, was to establish order in a savage or chaotic place.

Boots and Saddles

By showing Mexicans in the roles of retainers, dependents, comics, and incapable of defending themselves except with knives, Gene Autry's films reinforced established patterns for racial relations. In "Boots and Saddles" (1937), an autocratic English boy about twelve years old inherits a ranch somewhere in the Southwest. (The film was actually made near Lone Pine, California.) The boy arrives with his very English Solicitor and announces that he plans to sell the ranch to pay off ranch debts. His father had been a great friend of the cowboys, a very democratic man, and when alive hired numerous Mexican men and women to work on his ranch. The boy's English solicitor asks why the Mexican laborers have not been paying rent for their housing instead of being dependent upon the ranch owner to provide them with housing. Since the Solicitor serves as a comic foil, and is obviously out of touch with Western values, his suggestion can be nothing but ridiculous. The Mexican laborers are obviously *supposed* to be childlike people, dependent upon the owner of the ranch, supplanted, since the owner's death, by the foreman, Gene Autry.

However feudal such a system may seem, democratic values associated with the agrarian West are called upon to make judgments concerning the boy and his solicitor. The first day on the ranch the boy appears in English riding clothes and insists on riding a 'spirited' horse, against Autry's advice. The horse runs away with the boy but Autry (who plays in this film, as in all others in which he stars, under his own name) saves him and the boy promptly becomes his friend. When they get back to the ranch the solicitor has arranged a meeting with a villain who wants to buy the ranch in order to obtain the horses which run wild on it. He has a market for them with the Army at nearby Fort Wayne. When the hero elicits from the villain what his intentions are, Autry tells the boy that they can keep the ranch and sell the horses themselves. The villain, it turns out, holds a mortgage on the ranch. He announces that the boy must pay up within sixty days or lose everything.

Autry must fight to save the jobs of the poor Mexicans as well as the property of the boy while confronting the wiles of the villain and the cautious, civilized economic policy of the British solicitor. The cowboys and Gene launch a roundup of the wild horses, which they accomplish while singing in close harmony, which is perhaps appropriately expressive of the harmony they have with the land and their work. After the roundup, as they are riding toward the Fort where they will try to sell their horses, they are followed by a buggy in which an older man, dressed in city clothes, and a young woman, in modern dress, are riding. The older man rudely orders the cowboys to get out of the way. Once again the values of the Western, in this case the behavioral ideal of civility, are established as standards against which the behavior of those foreign to the West are judged. Since the man has been rude, the independent cowboys refuse—at first—to let him pass and the older man and the young woman (who turns out to be the man's daughter) get dust in their eyes. Frog (Smiley Burnette) sings a taunting song that further insults them before they finally are allowed to pass. The girl, irritated, vows to get even with Autry, the leader of the cowboys.

After they arrive at the Fort, and after Frog and the boy have played comic havoc with the company bugle, unwittingly giving orders to the troops, Autry goes to the company commander's home. The girl of the wagon answers his knock at the door. She is young and beautiful but has been cleaning house and is wearing an apron. Autry mistakes her for the maid. She lets Autry believe that she *is* the maid and agrees to go out with him to a Mexican restaurant for dinner. The implication seems to be that Autry is a common man, one who would likely feel on the same social level with a maid but not with the daughter of the company commander, which, of course, the girl turns out to be. They have dinner together and listen to Mexican music and then Autry sings. The young woman is friendly but does not tell Autry her true social position. The next day the commander finds that Autry's bid on the contract to provide horses for the Fort, made for the sake of the boy and the ranch (and the Mexican workers) is exactly equal to the villain's bid on the contract. The commander decides to have a horse race to settle the issue. The villain does everything possible to prevent Autry from succeeding, including having him served with a process and burning the barn where Autry's horses are kept, but Autry prevails, wins the race, and the villain is exposed. Autry and the girl ride back to the ranch where a Mexican *fiesta* celebrates the victory for the *peones* who had been in danger of losing their jobs. Harmony and order are re-established and celebrated in song.

Such a synopsis illustrates the assumed dependency of the Mexican laborers on Anglo employers and their representatives. The Englishman's values, presumably less democratic, ironically suggest that the Mexicans should be equal to the Anglo Americans, equal in responsibility and in position, while according to Autry's Western values, dependency is the natural state for Mexicans.

Mexicali Rose

"Mexicali Rose," released by Republic in 1939, as the title suggests, deals more overtly with frontier problems. The initial scenes focus viewer attention upon an often used incident in Gene Autry's films, whereby an element from the 'true' Western of action and cowboys and guns contrast with an 'entertainment' or artificial element from the musical Western. The contrast serves to juxtapose Autry's 'true' Western side, with his 'entertainment' side, and thereby establish the primacy of the former by making the 'entertainment' side appear foolish in one way or another. The action begins with a chase, a conventional element of the true Western, but the chase is to enable Autry to reach a radio station across the border in Mexico where he is to sing, evidently for a very enthusiastic radio audience, his version of the then popular song, "Mexicali Rose." On the way into the radio station he becomes comically entangled with a lovely young woman, Miss Laredo (Lu Ann Walters), thereby contrasting his somewhat foolish life as an entertainer with his cowboy skills as a rider.

The entanglement of Autry and Miss Laredo involves buttons which catch and tie them together even while he sings his romantic ballad on the radio. Afterwards Autry discovers that she is at the studio representing an orphanage endowed with the land where the Alta Vista Oil Company, whose promoter owns the radio station, has drilled a well. However, the company has paid no royalties of any sort to the orphanage and Miss Laredo is very angry. An aggressive, upper class young woman who apparently volunteers her efforts on behalf of the orphans, she accuses the villain of perpetrating a stock fraud through the oil company. When she discovers that Autry works for the radio station, and has even helped advertise stock in the Alta Vista Oil Company on his radio program, she is very angry with him. The villain wants Autry to sign a contract to continue singing for the station, but Autry, a serious cowboy in spite of his job as an entertainer, cannot sign until he determines if Miss Laredo's allegations are true. The villain tells Autry it is none of his business, but Autry's cowboy (as opposed to entertainer) side controls his behavior.

Frog (Smiley Burnette) and Autry (on horses, of course) ride to the site of the oil well to attempt to discover the truth, but they are intercepted by some of the villain's men. Autry and his comical friend then ride toward the orphanage but they are stopped by Valdéz (Noah Beery) and his gang of stereotypical Mexican *banditos,* reminiscent of unruly Mexican revolutionaries. The film neutralizes their revolutionary characteristics by treating them as comic relics from the past. Valdéz decides to steal Autry's horse and does so while Autry and Frog are visiting the orphanage. Autry gives chase and, of course, at a signal, the trained horse, Champion, rears and throws Valdéz from the saddle. Valdéz then takes Autry and his friend prisoners. That night, around the campfire, Valdéz listens to his favorite song, "Mexicali Rose," on a phonograph. A clumsy bandit breaks the record in the middle of the song and Autry, although tied up, begins to sing the rest of the song. Valdéz is entranced. He unties Autry and asks him to sing another song. Autry does—the song is about Robin Hood—and as he sings Valdéz suffers a conversion experience. He decides to live like Robin Hood—especially with the orphanage in mind. Valdéz, it should be noted, as well as the other bandits, all speak broken English with a little Spanish mixed in and all dress in disreputable and ragged Charro costumes. They are naive and childish. Autry is able to manipulate the morality of the revolutionary using a song about Robin Hood.

Released by the now reformed Valdéz, Autry and Frog go to the drilling site and discover that the Alta Vista Oil Company is hauling oil to the well site in order to trick investors into buying company stock. At the orphanage, which is run by a priest whose family holds a land grant from the Spanish throne to the orphanage property, Autry and Miss Laredo plan a benefit show in order to raise money for the Mexican children. Autry's entertainer side comes to the fore. Valdéz, reformed by Autry's song, steals from a promotional barbecue given by the oil company in order to bring food to the orphanage to be served at the benefit. During the benefit Valdéz forces people to contribute to the orphanage while two Mexican children do a very typical dance as part of the entertainment. With Autry's help the orphanage survives; the child-like Mexicans are assured a place for their children.

In the meantime, Autry and Frog have tricked the villain into flying to the well site. Worried, the villain tries to send his chief engineer back to the States since the engineer knows that the well is a fraud. The chief engineer rebels and goes to the orphanage. Autry and Frog recognize the chief engineer just as the villain's men take him away in a car. They give chase on their horses and save the man from being murdered. The engineer quickly reforms under Autry's influence and tells Autry that there may really be oil on the orphanage property and recommends a site for drilling. Autry, with the help of Valdéz, leaves oil traces in a stream near the new site, thereby tricking the villain into drilling a new well at that site. However, just as he is about to complete the project Autry's trick is discovered by Miss Laredo and the priest at the orphanage. They think Autry has tricked the people into further fraudulent investments and the police come to investigate. Frightened, the villain sells all of his stock in Alta Vista Oil to Autry. Realizing that he has been tricked, the villain tries to get the property back through force and trickery which leads to a gun fight and, eventually, to a chase once more involving Autry on his horse and the villain and his henchmen in a car. In the gun fight Valdéz loses his life, but otherwise all ends well; the other bandits/revolutionaries are arrested but promised lenient treatment in view of their reformation. The villains are arrested. Autry's benevolent company discovers oil. He saves the orphanage. Social order prevails in Mexico due to the efforts of Gene Autry. It is clear that such order would not have been possible without the intervention of the cowboy, who must be able to cross frontiers in order to take necessary action to impose social justice.

Rancho Grande

"Rancho Grande," released by Republic in 1940, like "Boots and Saddles," treats the familiar material of a ranch inherited by someone alien to Western values. The plot required Autry to bring those values to bear on the behavior of Kay and Tom Dodge (June Storey and Dick Hogan), who have inherited the ranch from their grandfather but have no love of the land or knowledge of ranching. They bring their young Eastern friends to the ranch, have loud parties, dance the jitterbug, and refuse to work. Autry, while patient, obviously provides a standard for more restrained, conventional behavior against which the young people are to be judged.

The film opens with a scene in which Mexican children are speaking and singing in Spanish, with Autry singing with them, also in Spanish, so it would seem to be in Mexico. Later we find out the action takes place near a town called Dodgeville, obviously named after the deceased grandfather, the *patrón* of the community. The children belong to the Mexican dependents of the ranch. The two young people, Kay and Tom Dodge, want to sell the ranch. The sale, however, will take away the jobs of the Mexican *peones* who are trying to install an irrigation system planned and begun by Kay and Tom's grandfather before his death. In order to get the money for the project the grandfather has mortgaged the ranch heavily. An evil lawyer, the representative of a large citrus company which holds the mortgage and wants the land, tries various mean tricks, including dynamiting the work site for the irrigation project, in order to frustrate Autry's efforts to complete the project.

However, the dynamite causes a rock slide that injures the old family retainer, José, and Tom and Kay, who have learned to love José, have a change of heart. Another dynamite trick closes the train tunnel that is bringing irrigation pipe to finish the job and save the ranch. Gene gets the "amigos" and "muchachos" of the ranch to ride to chase the villains away. They are successful and the ranch is saved. Led by Autry, an economic system which patterns Mexican laborers as the dependents of Anglo land owners, has been successfully defended. The cowboy image provides an easy shorthand in place of a thoughtful examination of the relations between ethnic groups and nations.

One scene, which tends to catch the tone of the film, involves a christening. Mexican women, dressed in typical village costumes of the nineteenth century, ask Kay, dressed in typical, somewhat voluminous shorts typical of the 1940s in the United States, to be the godmother of a newborn Mexican child on the ranch. She finds the idea amusing, but in her shorts—far too unconventional and improper for the West— she offends Gene and Frog's Western sense of modesty, so she wraps a table cloth around her and goes to the church. At the church the Mexican family has about twenty children and the little girl who is to be baptized is given at least fifteen names—which, in the interest of innocent comedy, holds the Latin American legal and cultural custom of retaining both maternal and paternal names, and thereby lengthening the complete name, to the standard of the shorter, Anglo naming custom. The Mexican women effusively express their gratitude to the beautiful blond Kay for condescending to be the godmother. However, the baptism scene is handled tastefully and with restraint—if one can ignore the comic stereotyping and ingratiating and servile attitude of the players acting as Mexicans.

Gene, and later, Roy Rogers and other cowboy stars, in their film fictions, all helped to colonize in other lands, particularly in Latin America. Their task was to help the colonists of Latin America (and, at least on one occasion, in Canada) to achieve stability and order and then, as in the traditional Western, move on, not personifying the power their conquest had given them as they would have had they been *caudillos* instead of cowboys. Obviously, such scenarios had international political implications.

South of the Border

"South of the Border," released in 1939 by Republic, has an overt political (and colonial) message, and it found considerable favor among the public. As Phil Hardy notes, the success of this film "firmly committed its star to the war effort (even though the United States had not yet committed itself)..." (97). Introducing the film for *Melody Ranch Theater,* a television series featuring his films, Autry said that it was one of his biggest pictures, that translated into Spanish it was popular in Mexico and Spain and, in English, was one of the favorite films for the then young Princess Elizabeth of England. Pat Buttram, who often played the role of the comic alongside Autry and who appeared with Autry on the television show, noted that this was the film that got Autry into downtown theaters. Evidently Autry's fans found it comforting to think of their cowboy hero as an international peace keeper, especially in Latin America.

The film opens with a song about a fiesta, very harmonic, in a Mexican town. Frog and Autry decide to go to the fiesta, which promises considerable musical entertainment, but first Autry must establish himself as a 'serious' cowboy: he must report to the consulate since he is working undercover as a Federal Agent, a not at all unusual role for cowboys such as Gene Autry and Roy Rogers in the early 1940s. Near the consulate Autry sees Dolores (Lupita Tovar), the daughter of a wealthy family, and he is immediately taken by her beauty. Meanwhile Patsy (Mary Lee), a young, apparently Mexican, orphan, provides comic interest by adopting Autry as her father and following him everywhere, against his genial wishes.

At the consulate Autry learns that foreign agents are trying to start a revolution in a Latin America country south of Mexico in order to get a submarine base and access to the country's oil. Autry, as a secret agent, must go to the country, get rid of the foreign agents, and establish order. Autry and Frog and the Cass County Boys, his musical cohorts, gallop their horses on board a ship bound for Palermo, the name given to the Latin American country they must ride to save. Once there Autry will meet the uncle of Dolores, Don Diego (Frank Reicher), who is a cattleman and businessman in the area, and attempt to find out the identity of the foreign agents.

Lois (June Storey), a pretty blond nightclub singer, is also on board the ship. Since she has been helped by the head of the foreign agents by being given a job to sing in his nightclub in Palermo, she has agreed, somehow innocently, to smuggle $200,000.00 into Palermo which is to be used by the agent to fund revolutionary efforts. The little orphan girl, who has adopted Autry as her father, stows away on the ship and accidentally sees Lois hide the money inside one of Autry's suitcases. Lois fears that her own suitcases will be searched at customs, but somehow knows that Autry's will be immune. Patsy, the little girl, takes the money and hides it inside her doll, deciding to keep it in case Autry sends her back to Mexico and she needs money to return to Palermo to be near him.

At customs Autry and Frog have some problems, but Don Diego, (Dolores' uncle) vouches for him and the word of the wealthy man serves to open the country to Autry's investigations. Later, Don Diego notes that "We were good friends with the United States. Then foreign propaganda led workers astray." Andreo (Duncan Renaldo), Don Diego's nephew and the brother of the beautiful Dolores, has been led astray by the foreign propaganda and is a leader of the so called liberators. Andreo, like Gene, wears an anachronistic costume, an elegant charro outfit. Gene, of course, is costumed as an elegant cowboy. The foreign agent, and Don Diego, wear contemporary business suits.

Andreo is a dashing and sympathetic character but depicted as politically naive. Learning that Lois has hidden the money intended to fund his revolutionary cause in Autry's luggage, he demands it, but of course Autry knows nothing of the money, which is still hidden in the doll.

At first Don Diego's *vaqueros* don't want to help Autry but then he sings for them. Naive and simple, they love music and Autry wins their allegiance. Capable of using modern technology as well as the musical skills of a cowboy hero, Autry deciphers and sends messages electronically using the Morse code and loads cattle by swimming them to the boat to enable Don Diego to get them to market. He protects United States political interests as well as property interests in Palermo. In a final shoot-out, the leader of the foreign agents is shot and the little girl's doll is thrown over a cliff. All of the money falls out and Andreo's band of liberators, the revolutionaries, chase the money (indicating their greed, which evidently, fuels their revolutionary ardor). Andreo, the misguided young revolutionary and Dolores' brother, also dies in the battle.

Autry rides off, singing "South of the Border," but unfortunately, by the time he rides all the way back to Mexico, where they left the beautiful Dolores, she has become a nun (as the lyrics of the song suggest) and the old priest explains to Autry (as the music continues) that she was shamed by her brother's revolutionary actions and feels she must do penance by giving her life to the church. Autry rides away again, continuing with the song. The sentimental ballad, pleasantly sung, does not account for the action in the film, wherein a United States agent goes, in an undercover role, into a Latin American country and uses force to protect the interests of the United States as well as the interests of the property owners in that country—interests which, evidently, are one and the same. The beautiful Latin American woman has been saved, in a sense, from a life of shame and the child-like Latin American people have not been allowed to let misguided revolutionaries lead them astray. Order established, Autry moves on to new frontiers.

Revolutions, it should be noted, have not been very popular in the United States, and Latin American revolutions have enjoyed very little enthusiasm. They are judged against the standard of the American Revolution, a model which did not *go too far*. Autry's films rhetorically neutralize Latin American revolutions by making revolutionaries naive romantics, like Andreo in "South of the Border" or comic *banditos*, like Valdéz in "Mexicali Rose."

Down Mexico Way

In "Down Mexico Way," released in 1941 by Republic, Autry protects the property interests of the 'little' people in Sage City, U.S.A. and of a wealthy family in San Ramón, Mexico from big city criminal types obviously foreign to Western values. He also demonstrates that revolutionaries in Mexico are but comic braggarts who, with a little indulgence, can be taught that their best interests lie in protecting private property and maintaining the old order.

To establish himself as the kind of man who can be trusted by both the widows of Sage City as well as the *hacendados* of San Ramón, Autry illustrates the importance of clean living. During his introduction to the film on *Melody Ranch Theater,* Autry recalled that the movie opened with some "fellows drinking beer." The film actually opens with a party, on Gene's ranch near Sage City, and the drinking comes from barrels ostentatiously labeled *cider* while the guests sing a popular song of the day, "The Beer Barrel Polka."

Apparently they have reason for harmony in Sage City since Mayor Tubbs (Andrew Tombes) has signed an agreement with two men posing as Hollywood producers. They are going to make a Western, somewhat like "Dodge City" or "Virginia City," they say, using Sage City as the locale. During the party, the phony Hollywood producers announce, reading from a phony telegram, that John Wayne has agreed to star in the film. The allusions to Hollywood Westerns, as well as the villains who, dressed in city clothes, represent Hollywood artificiality, authenticate Autry's character, that of a respected rancher living near a small town, a man who embodies agrarian, Western, values. Later in the film, after they have crossed the frontier into Mexico, Autry and his 'sidekicks' arrive at the hacienda of the wealthy Don Alvarado in a Model T taxi while Don Alvarado's daughter and her *dueña* arrive in an elegant, late model car. Such references to the worlds of entertainment and wealth, so important to the musical Western, contrast with the true Western cowboy element in an Autry picture, and thereby attest to Autry's credentials as a cowboy hero, in spite of his ability to sing.

The phony Hollywood producers have tricked the townspeople, one, at least, a poor old widow dressed in black, into investing in their project which they have no intention of completing. After the party at Autry's ranch the swindlers depart for Mexico where they are going to meet with even bigger criminals who are out to take money from the people of San Ramón, Mexico, using the same trick they had used in Sage City. However, while cleaning up after the party, Autry and Frog and Pancho Grande (Harold Huber) discover the truth from the scrap of paper which had served as the spurious telegram concerning John Wayne. A series of telegrams follow to Hollywood concerning the two producers. Soon the townspeople realize they have been swindled. Autry and Frog and Pancho leave for Mexico to recover the money.

Harold Huber plays Pancho Grande with a lot of grease paint and a very phony accent. He has been hired, by Frog, while posing as the best Mexican cook north of the border, and he promises that he is well known all over Mexico. As it turns out, unknown to Autry and Frog, he is a comic opera revolutionary in hiding in the United States from Mexican authorities. A braggart, he is a traditional comic type. By making the revolutionary child-like and foolish, the film fortifies the stereotype of the Latin American as child-like and foolish, especially when the Latin American wants to change governments—to rebel—and thereby cause everyone a great deal of trouble. The image of the cowboy, again, provided an easy way to avoid thought about the complex problem of social justice in Latin America as well as about the United States' role in maintaining systems of government which did not lead to social justice.

The three men have scarcely begun the trip when Pancho tries to fix Autry's car and fails, so they must ride their horses, towing the car, into Mexico. Pancho's expertise, and lack of credibility, contrast with Autry's restraint and honesty. Once across the border, they decide to take the train to San Ramón. On the train Autry meets the beautiful Maria Elena (Fay McKenzie) who speaks Spanish with considerable skill. After an impromptu musical number, she tells Autry that she is going home to San Ramón to make a movie with the same producers who have, unknown to her, swindled the citizens of Sage City. Autry tells her of the Sage City crime and that he is looking for the producers, Flood and Gerard, (Murray Alper and Arthur Loft). Maria Elena thinks Autry is wrong but invites him to her wealthy father's hacienda to meet the producers.

At the hacienda Pancho Grande, the revolutionary with, we are to suppose, a price upon his head, is afraid to confront Don Alvarado, Maria's father (Julian Rivero), a figure of wealth and authority. Autry and Frog go in and meet the Hollywood producers, but since the two swindlers who posed as producers in Sage City have deferred to more important swindlers in San Ramón, Autry does not meet the men he expected to meet and decides that he was mistaken. However, once outside, when they see the luxurious Hollywood producer's car and identify it as the car driven by the Sage City swindlers, they decide to stay on in San Ramón.

In San Ramón they enjoy a typical Hollywood-Mexican fiesta. The Herrara Sisters sing "Guadalajara," and there is a mélange of dancing and costumes. Pancho, with Autry and Frog, meets Captain Rodriguez (Thornton Edwards) as once again the film recalls Pancho's wild past as a revolutionary. Captain Rodriguez, however, merely tells Pancho to behave himself.

The next day Autry, Frog and Pancho try to go to the movie set, on location in the desert, to make sure the production is authentic. They are not permitted to go near, but they are able to jump their horses over a fence. They gallop down and steal Maria Elena away from the set. A chase follows, but they escape to a cave known by Pancho. Autry's cowboy heroics place him on the wrong side of the law, even though he is obviously fighting for the right. As in non-musical Westerns, he must use the ways of the survivor, often violent, in order to protect the weak, even if the weak are unable to perceive the need for violence. He convinces Maria Elena that she must convince her father, who is going to provide $500,000 to make the movie, to wait. She follows Gene's counsel and her father, at the contract signing, demands that the producers, as a sign of good faith, put up one fourth of the money. They don't have the money, but plan to rob the train bringing the $500,000 to San Ramón from Mexico City, thereby stealing Don Alvarado's money to present it as their share.

Autry, meanwhile, hunted as a criminal, must hide out at the cave with Frog and Pancho. Juan, (Duncan Renaldo) one of Pancho's old cohorts, brings one of the villain's hired men, bound and gagged and hidden in straw on the bottom of a wagon pulled by a burro, to the cave. Autry wants the man to tell them the plans of the Hollywood swindlers. After Juan and Pancho have thrown knives at him, getting closer and closer, demonstrating the stereotypical knife wielding skills of Mexicans, Autry decides to try his hand. A comic scene follows wherein Pancho and Juan pretend to teach Autry how to throw the knife and he pretends to be a novice. Finally the tactic works and the villain (unfamiliar with the ways of the Western and therefore unaware that Autry is as expert with the knife as the Mexicans) confesses that the swindlers intend to steal Don Alvarado's money from the train.

Pancho rides to get his old gang of revolutionaries—a barber, a baker, a grocery store owner and so forth—together. They all have old, ragged charro costumes ready, which identify them as former revolutionaries. So costumed, they ride to stop the swindlers and save the wealthy Don Alvarado's money. Whereas it might be assumed that former revolutionaries would not protect a *hacendado* such as Don Alvarado, it is evident that there is no class conflict in this film. Everybody looks after everybody else. The revolutionaries protect the wealthy.

The money, conveniently, comes by way of a van rather than a train. The villains attack the van from their horses and steal the money. Autry and Frog are soon hot in pursuit of the criminals, while Pancho and his old revolutionaries are hot on the trail of Autry, and the police, on motorcycles, chase Pancho, who they think is leading some sort of uprising. The chase leads to a shoot-out as Autry leads Pancho's revolutionaries in the battle which culminates in a fist fight between Autry and one of the villains. The police arrive on their motorcycles and try to arrest everybody, but Autry explains.

Autry and his friends ride after the swindlers who are on their way to the Sonora airport to fly back to the United States and escape. Autry's horsemanship—he is able to take a shortcut—enables him to catch the villains and he drops from a rock, rather high in the air in a most improbable way, into the back seat of the open convertible. He manages to knock the two most important swindlers out of the car, after considerable fist fighting, and as he is about to be shot by the driver, the driver is shot by someone chasing from behind, evidently one of the Mexican policemen. Autry leaps from the moving car just as it goes over a cliff.

The wealth of Don Alvarado has been saved as well as the life savings of the widows and farmers back at Sage City. At an elaborate farewell party for Autry and Frog, everybody sings "Down Mexico Way," in a blend of Spanish and English. The harmony is appropriate. Maria Elena invites Gene to return for a really big fiesta in San Ramón later and Gene accepts, but this time he and Smiley ride away singing. Pancho appears in the uniform of a policeman. The old revolutionary has become a police recruit. The comic reduction of the revolutionary assures the viewer that the days of social unrest in Mexico are far behind modern reality.

Gene Autry served in the Armed Forces during World War II, so his film career was interrupted for four years. Once back in Hollywood, however, he again began to make the kind of films which had made him popular before the war. One such film type was the musical Western set in a border town or, on occasion, in Mexico. Such films formed a major element in his film repertoire. Two such films were "Twilight on the Rio Grande" and "The Big Sombrero."

Twilight on the Rio Grande

"Twilight on the Rio Grande," released in 1947 by Republic, reflects a shift in the relationship between Mexico and the United States between the early 1940s, when the Good Neighbor policy was being stressed, to a slightly less friendly, post World War II relationship. The concerns of the film are not openly political, although it does present an argument for the right of a United States citizen to use weapons to seek justice in Mexico.

The film opens in a border town as we see Dusty (Bob Steele) lurking in the shadows of rather sinister surroundings. A 1946 (new, of course, at the time) Ford convertible pulls up the narrow, rain drenched street. Dusty either gets in or is abducted; the camera angle leaves the question of his volition unanswered. In the shadows, Torres, (Nacho Galindo) a Mexican man dressed in white, observes.

The next morning Autry and the Cass County Boys, who are given to breaking into song frequently, come down from their hotel room looking for Dusty, Autry's ranch partner. It is not clear what Autry and his friends are doing in Mexico, whether on business or pleasure, but soon they are involved in a criminal investigation. Mucho Pesos (Martin Garralaga), a seedy bum who seems to be willing to do anything for a peso, which Autry always flips to him in a patronizing manner, tells them their friend is at the police station. They go there to find Dusty dead.

Autry, intent upon investigating the murder of his friend, asks the police captain for permission to carry a gun in order to search for the killer who put a knife into Dusty's back. The police captain urges Autry to go back to his ranch and let the police take care of the problem. Autry refuses, but doesn't get permission to carry a gun.

That night, as he and his comic sidekick, Pokie (Sterling Holloway) are looking into the crime, a knife comes sailing out of the dark, thrown from a balcony, and just misses Autry. Autry climbs from his horse onto the balcony and charges into the room of Elena Del Rio (Adele Mara), who sings in a cantina owned by Jake Short (Howard J. Negley). Elena seems to want to avoid talking with Autry, and does so, even when confronted with the knife thrown at him. The next day she once again avoids talking with Autry. Eventually he sneaks into Elena's hacienda and finds her praying in the patio.

Elena talks openly to Autry in the security of her home, telling him that her father, a respected medical doctor with a practice on both sides of the border, had been found mysteriously killed with a knife. She is an upper class girl but has taken the job in the cantina in order to find out about her father's murder. She has not wanted to be seen talking openly to Autry for fear of being discovered. She explains that there is a large colony of war refugees living in the area and that they must sell their jewels in order to survive. The jewel buyers then smuggle the jewelry into the states where they can get a better price.

Autry, in spite of the admonition of the police, discovers, through a ruse with Elena's jewelry, that a lawyer, Henry Blackstone (Charles Evans), leads the smuggling ring that is exploiting the refugees. He breaks into Blackstone's office but Blackstone catches him and holds him under his gun. The villain then orders his men to kill Autry, making it look as if they shot him while he was trying to escape following a burglary attempt. Blackstone calls the police and charges Autry with the crime of burglary.

Autry and Pokie and the Cass County Boys are not shot, but they are arrested, presumably because the police think they are a gang. The police reveal that Torres, the shadowy man in the white suit, is an undercover policeman, and that the police themselves have been working hard to trap the jewel smugglers. Even Mucho Pesos, the comic relief early in the film, turns out to be a special investigator. Nothing in the shadowy border town is what it appears to be, and the genial and open faced Autry seems out of his element.

Mucho and Elena confront the villains before the police are ready to move in. Elena is knocked out and a United States ambulance is called. Mucho is shot, but not killed. Blackstone, the villain, decides to send the jewelry he has bought from the refugees along with Elena in the ambulance through to the United States. Autry, released from jail, unarmed but at least aware that the police suspect Blackstone, sees through the ruse. A bar room brawl ensues and Jake Short, the second ranking villain, tries to escape in a laundry truck. Autry chases him on Champion, promising certain, Western retribution, which follows when the villain wrecks the truck and falls, in the accident, upon his own knife. A final musical evening takes place at *El Molina Verde*, a cantina, in which Elena and Autry perform.

The Mexican police in the border town, with Autry's help, have caught the jewel thieves and solved the murder of Autry's ranch partner, who evidently had stumbled upon the criminals in the act. "Twilight on the Rio Grande," less political than earlier, more comic treatments of the Autry cowboy-in-Mexico film, has a dark, almost sinister and bitter, tone. Mexico scarcely seems to be the vacation paradise or the comedic banana republic Autry's prewar films depicted, perhaps because attitudes toward Mexico had changed, or perhaps simply because it was a musical Western with a detective story embedded, and, as such, required camera work and situations that seemed more threatening.

The Big Sombrero

In "The Big Sombrero," released in 1949 by Gene Autry Productions and Columbia Pictures, Autry starred in his first color film, according to his comments when introducing the film for *Melody Ranch Theater*. The color was no doubt a new element, but the film returned to the technique and theme of Autry's prewar border and Mexican films. Once more the action gently chides Autry's persona as an entertainer in order to authenticate his persona as a cowboy. Once more true Western values are used as standards for judging idle, wealthy young people who must learn how to behave, and once more Autry, as cowboy, must ensure internal order and property rights in a Latin American country.

"The Big Sombrero" opens as Autry sings a range ballad while sitting in a saddle. Throughout the song the viewer assumes that Autry is on a horse somewhere in a wilderness area. However, as he finishes the song, he steps from the saddle and the viewer realizes that Autry has been sitting in front of a painting of a western landscape, that he is actually in a pawn shop in a border town. The effect emphasizes the artificiality of the singing cowboy and establishes, as in the earlier films wherein this device was used, a comic perspective that will defuse the viewer's sense of irony concerning entertainers as cowboys, as well as his sense of irony concerning the anachronism of a cowboy, supposedly dressed as nineteenth century cowboy involved in a twentieth century setting with telephones, automobiles, and all 'normal' people dressed in contemporary clothing. Values remain constant in an Autry film, but time marches forward.

Autry is in the pawn shop because his traveling western show has gone bankrupt and he must pawn his guitar to get money to feed his horse. Once outside the pawn shop he runs into an old friend, a woman who has played in shows as a sort of Annie Oakley. She too has had to leave a traveling western show and is working as a *dueña* for Señorita Estrellita Estrada (Elena Verdugo), who is not only young and beautiful but wealthy, having inherited a large ranch in her native country, Mexico. Another old show business worker, James Garland (Stephen Dunne) manages the ranch for the young woman while trying to get her to marry him. He is a good looking city man, obviously not a true man of the West, so in spite of his ties with a traveling western show, he doesn't know anything about ranch work and needs a ranch foreman.

Autry goes to see him and accepts the job as ranch foreman, but soon discovers that Garland and Ben McBride (Gene Stutenroth) are trying to force the *campesinos,* the small farmers that live and run cattle and work as dependents on the young woman's property, to give up their homes and to give the villains their cattle in payment for the back rent which they have been unable to pay. The dependents of the ranch are in arrears because they have been unable to sell their cattle in their nearest market, the United States, due to a ban on importation of livestock after an outbreak of the hoof and mouth disease in Mexico. The restriction against selling cattle in the United States has been lifted and thus the cattle have become valuable to the villains. However, if the *campesinos* can only get their cattle to the market, across the border, they can pay their rent and keep their homes and livelihoods.

Autry, of course, immediately sides with them just as all true Western heroes side with small colonists, and, at a fiesta, the *campesinos* and Autry agree that they will drive the cattle north on horses, since the villains have been able to block their access to the railroad. Autry leads them on the cattle drive, demonstrating his survival skills as a cowboy.

In the meantime, Estrellita Estrada, the young woman who has inherited the ranch, doesn't like ranch life, preferring a glamorous life on the United States side of the border. She doesn't know about social conditions among the poor on her land. Autry tries to convince her to be more aware of her social responsibilities to the *campesinos.* His democratic Western values are, perhaps, somewhat strangely applied in the defense of feudalism, but nevertheless the young woman refuses to be responsible.

Finally, during the cattle drive, one of the villains shoots an innocent

Mexican boy. When they bring his body to the ranch the young woman realizes she has been foolish and vows to change. One villain, Garland, formerly of the western show, is allowed to escape, although the other villain, McBride, is shot by the Mexican boy in his dying moments. All ends happily as Señorita Estrada assumes responsibility for her *campesinos*. Autry, a true man of the Westerns in spite of his entertainment background, has been able to bring order out of chaos for rich and poor Mexicans alike. He rides into the sunset, letting the viewer assume that the order he has established will somehow be permanent.

Plot synopsis, such as of the films discussed, illustrates how racism and international dependency were inherent in the image of Gene Autry's singing cowboy. Because the Mexicans are child-like, Autry must interfere. Because the people of Palermo are misguided revolutionaries, Autry must interfere. The plots explain the necessity for United States' interference in Latin American affairs as a means to impose political order in that part of the world. Gene Autry's films were widely accepted. Autry was often among the ten top money-making stars during his career. (Fenin and Everson 213). One year he made it to fourth place in that category of film actors. Such popularity is a measure of the widespread acceptance of the frontier ideology in his films, an ideology which those films shared with most other Westerns which dealt with relations between nations in the Americas.

As an old man, introducing his films on *Melody Ranch Theater*, Autry seems an amiable gentleman, proud that he has been an inspiration to generations of people who believe that he embodies the behavioral ideals for the cowboy in his films. His character never abused alcohol nor any other drug. His character fought fair. His character did not steal nor cheat. His character was altruistic. Certainly, Gene Autry, the man, never connived with his writers, nor did his writers or his producers ever connive with anyone else, to promote an expansionist frontier policy by reinforcing racist attitudes which would lend support to United States' involvement in foreign lands, and especially to the assumption that it is the duty of the United States to order Latin American internal and external affairs according to the moral vision of United States' leaders. Such an ideology was inherent in the popular Western, the form which Autry's writers used as a vehicle for Autry's personality. A gentle man, it is highly unlikely Gene Autry ever dreamed, or dreams, that the stories he appeared in, either in film, on television, or in the comics, could have had any harmful effects on anyone in the world. Yet today, it is likely, his affable blend of song and knight errantry, so effective as a means of communicating the ideology of the Western, has had serious repercussions indeed in parts of Latin America as well as in the United States.

Chapter V
The *Caudillo's* Ordered World in Popular Culture

The Comedia Ranchera *and Traditional Order*

Gene Autry's films assume that Anglo cowboy heroes have the right—the duty, in fact—to cross frontiers when it is necessary to establish order. Such action should require considerable reflection; the sovereignty of governments should not be taken lightly. Nevertheless, the images from such films, from fictions by writers like Louis L'Amour, as well as from television and comic books, far too often supplant rational thought about ways people from different cultures and nations should relate to each other. Unfortunately, in Latin America, widely consumed and distributed narratives offer images which, like the images of the cowboy in the United States, often displace rational examination about life on frontiers.

As was seen in the discussion of the novels of M.L. Estefanía, and as will be seen in a discussion of the comic book series, *Aquila Solitaria*, popular literature in Latin America frequently images the frontier zone as all but nearly uninhabitable. In other fictions, such as in the soon to be examined comic book, *El cacique*, indigenous people can and do live in the hinterlands in peace—in fact, in an Edenic innocence that can only exist outside time—as long as intruders leave them alone. For that reason it is more attractive for many people in Latin America to identify themselves with the hinterlands than with centers of civilization. As Carlos Rangel, the Venezualan intellectual, so persuasively argues in *Del buen salvage al buen revolucionario [From the Nobel Savage to the Nobel Revolutionary]*, to be a noble revolutionary in contemporary Latin America is, axiomatically, to be a Nobel Savage, the descendant of Native Americans and necessarily from the hinterlands.

In the popular works to be examined in this chapter, indigenous people find contact with 'outsiders' dangerous. People in popular works who cross frontiers risk contamination from other cultures, while immigrants are frequently seen as invaders or as people who were rejected as undesirable in their own land. Returning emigrants inspire distrust.

Indeed, in Latin American tradition and history, the power of the *caudillo* of the hinterlands stems from his close contact with people whose lives have *not* been disordered by contact with other cultures.

69

Ironically, as we shall see, since the wars of independence, many Latin American *caudillos* have depended for their power upon financial support from Europe or the United States.

At any rate, in many popular fictions, Latin America sees the frontier image as a stockade; fear and distrust are the issue of a stockade mentality about frontiers. Since barbarous intruders threaten order and civilization, popular Latin American frontier narratives look inward from frontiers toward village, regional or national centers of power, and more inward still, to the heroic individual who incorporates all space and time within his own ego and, by total domination, brings order and stability.

Order and stability deny change. New people and new experience bring change. Thus change brought by frontiersmen endangers the *caudillo*. The local or national *caudillo* promises order and strength, which, both in popular fictions as well as in reality, may be imposed in a violent, cruel fashion as long as it achieves the desirable end of maintaining order. In this way, image literature—such as cinema, comic books, and television—frequently ratifies the need for *caudillaje*.

The popular frontier film genre, the *Comedia Ranchera*, with its idealized stories about Latin American hinterlands, would seem to be innocently unaware of the sinister world of *caudillos*. A traditional *Comedia Ranchera* is a song filled film about life in the provinces. One scholar has suggested that they are influenced by the song filled films of Roy Rogers and Gene Autry (Ayala Blanco 64-66). But while the films of Gene Autry and Roy Rogers are filled with anachronisms which enable frontier values to be brought to bear upon contemporary events, a *Comedia Ranchera*, in at least the older versions, is closed to time and space. The films celebrate specific regions where beautiful girls maintain their virtue in costumes from the colonial past, and handsome men, dressed as wealthy ranchers from the same period, celebrate the customs and beauty of the provinces. *Ay qué rechulo es Puebla [Oh How Lovely is Puebla], Qué lindo es Michoacán, [How Beautiful is Michoacán]* and *Solo Veracruz es bello [Only Veracruz is Beautiful]* exemplify the genre. Such films idealize a provincial world of cock fights, horse races, songs, mariachi groups, and tavern brawls (Ayala Blanco 68).

The titles suggest a representation of specific geography. Yet, just as the traditional *Comedia Ranchera* exists outside history, so it also exists outside space. The heroes of the *Comedia Ranchera* have only vague, hinterland nationalities; they may be identified as more or less idealized Mexican *Charros*, or idealized Venezuelan *Llaneros* [Plainsmen] or idealized Argentine *Gauchos* (Ayala Blanco 69).

While the *Comedia Ranchera,* full of songs and innocent pleasures, celebrates provincial life, it also underscores the need for the strong hand of a *caudillo* to maintain peace in such a world. The films look back with longing to the stable and tranquil world when Porfirio Diaz ruled

Mexico with the help of a paternalistic oligarchy. They are rooted in the semifeudal hacienda system where the class struggle is resolved in gratitude and generosity (Ayala Blanco 68). Since outsiders bring change, and since the *Comedia Ranchera* resists change, the genre conveys a frontier ideology which opposes intrusion by those from outside the culture.

Life in the hinterlands depicted in the traditional *Comedia Ranchera* may not be as barbarous as that depicted in many Latin America fictions and histories; nevertheless, fist and gun fights fill many a reel. In recent years a bloody and violent variation of the *Comedia Ranchera*, perhaps influenced by Italian Westerns, has emerged. In such films the frontier becomes extremely barbaric. Usually such films allow contemporary events and social problems, such as the plight of illegal aliens crossing into the United States or living in the United States, or the evils and dangers of drug smuggling, to be depicted along with innocent country girls in old fashioned dresses (usually seen in strong contrast with city— or Anglo American—girls of doubtful virtue). In such films, just as in the films of Gene Autry, country values are used to correct city ways. The values of the provinces still govern, and the ultimate theme resists change, either from crossing the frontier or having the frontier crossed. Such films do, however, recognize change in time, something the older films refuse to acknowledge.

The Caudillo *and Sexual Possession*

The audience for pornography is relatively classless. Pornography, we would all like to think, is not enjoyed by anyone we know or have anything to do with, yet it seems to find its way among all kinds of people. Newspapers love to report the scandal when ministers, noted businessmen, celebrities and civic leaders are caught viewing a forbidden pornographic movie. Yet there are, doubtless, many in the audience from all walks of life, dishwashers, parking lot attendants, college professors, and other workers of the world. Pornography, it seems, appeals across class, educational, and social lines. Therefore, an "adults only" comic book about a frontier indicates the degree of omniscience of the stockade mentality among Latin American readers toward frontiers as well as readers' covert admiration for the sexual prowess, appetite, and dominance of a *caudillo*.

The comic book, *"El cacique"* (January 4, 1974) tells the story of a '*cacique,*' a rural *caudillo* whose power doesn't extend as far as a national *caudillo*. In this comic the small town *cacique*, either Creole or Spaniard, ventures as a frontiersman into an innocent, isolated, village. He learns to speak the language of the Native Americans, wins their confidence, then exploits them by buying their art and then, more to the point for an adults only comic book, violates the women of the village.

Illustration One: *"El Cacique,"* 113 "The Chiapaneca women," we are told in the legend, "of unusual beauty, attract him because of the warm color of their skin." The intruder promises: "If you do what I ask I will give you a pretty gift."

SUS OJOS PROFANOS SE DELEITARON MUCHAS OCASIONES AL CON-
TEMPLARLAS BAÑÁNDOSE EN EL FRESCO RÍO.

Illustration Two: *"El Cacique,"* 5 The *cacique* first contaminates the village with his eyes, watching the young women while they innocently bathe, as in illustration two. In morally indignant tones the narrator tells us that "His [the *cacique's*] profane eyes were delighted on many occasions contemplating them [the young women] bathing themselves in the cool river."

As one might guess, that is only the beginning as we go about the business of pornography. That business involves a great deal of sex and voyeurism, which seems to be a hereditary affliction in this comic book.

The narrator seems not at all disturbed that the reader's profane eyes feast upon the same bathers. Later the *cacique* is watched by his son as he assaults the wife of one of his workers, an incident which leads the boy, and the happy reader, into an orgy of watching. The degenerate *cacique* not only contaminates the morality of the village, but by watching, intrudes into the most private acts of the people. The outsider assumes the right to intrude wherever he wishes to intrude. His power and person go everywhere; he possesses the women, first with his eyes and later through sex.

Of course the pornographic comic book doesn't really end; the voyeuristic sexual activity repeats itself, according to the laws of pornography described by Steven Marcus, until it fills the required number of pages. But however formless pornography may be in a literary sense, it certainly is not without moral form. Immoral acts could not be depicted if the audience did not share some standard of morality violated by the story. One moral standard is the sexual innocence of the village prior to the advent of the frontiersman. The myth of the Garden—and the innocence therein—is related to the myth of the fall of man from innocence as well as to our civilized belief that sexual acts should be private acts. The comic book assumes that prior to the arrival of the frontiersman the village lived without knowledge of sin; after his arrival the moral rule of sexual privacy must exist in the now fallen world, but of course the comic book delights in breaking that rule.

Illustration Three: *"El Cacique"* 21 Celestino, the son of the small town *cacique,* is "tremendously surprised when he saw his father forcing himself upon the woman of Anastasio," one of his father's employees. "Quiet," the *cacique* orders the woman. "It's better if you don't act like you don't want to!"

The *cacique* assumes that he not only has the right to possess the women as a voyeur, but also that he has the right to possess them as sexual partners. When grown, the boy continues as a voyeur and takes his father's place as the sexually dominant male in the village.

The implicit rule for frontiers violated in this pornographic fantasy mandates a necessary barrier between European and Native American cultures, a barrier which will prevent the lascivious frontiersman from knowing and possessing all. The reader, once sated with images of voluptuous, scantily clad maidens, all forced—if not willing or even eager—to give their favors to the *cacique,* will likely put the comic aside and affirm a public morality in favor of keeping village traditions pure from cultural contamination. However, the same reader has obviously enjoyed a sexual fantasy in which he has savored the power of the *cacique* who has those favors at his will. The indigenous people monopolize morality and foreigners violate morality. The *cacique* assumes the ultimate form of personal power—sexual possession—the basic act of the comic, repeated over and again until the last page.

Illustration Four: *"El Cacique"* 24 "What a turn on," he exclaims as he watches (see illustration four) a young man and his girl. "What an appetite this damned Indian has! I like her...I will have her!"

REVISTA

AGUILA SOLITARIA

El hijo de las águilas
lucha por la justicia
y la libertad de su raza.
¡Vive sus aventuras!

Cómprala
cada semana
en tu puesto de
revistas favorito

Illustration Five: *Aquila Solitaria* From this picture on the inside front cover, one may see that Aquila Solitaria, fiercely indigenous, would seem to be Mestizo with at least some of the blood of the conquistadors in his veins.

The Caudillo *and Personal Order:*
Aquila Solitaria
Aquila Solitaria [Lone Eagle], first produced and distributed in Mexico by Editora K. under the direction of Modesto Vazquez González, is now being produced for Caribbean, Central, and South American readers by Editora Cinco, S.A., under the direction of Pedro Vargas G., of Bogõtá, Colombia. More than 800 comic books have now appeared in the series, about half of which were available for this study. A frontier

adventure story, *Aquila Solitaria* apparently appeals to what one would consider the traditional, Latin American, comic book audience, an audience made up of people of both sexes with elementary and high school educations. One would assume that the readers were predominantly young, but it is likely that many people of various ages read *Aquila Solitaria*. Like *El cacique, Aquila Solitaria* contains a liberal dose of pornography, which probably widens its appeal.

Widely distributed and read throughout Latin America, *Aquila Solitaria* reinforces concepts of the frontier based upon many attitudes found in Spanish and early day Latin American history and myth. *Aquila Solitaria* thus forms a means for understanding grounded in traditional culture. *Aquila Solitaria* helps to buttress cultural patterns for thought which enable its audience to understand contemporary experience, such as the presence of Anglo Americans in their countries, for the culture industry conditions them to judge new historical experience in the light of the patterns which they experience imaginatively through their reading.

Among other things, *Aquila Solitaria* dramatizes attitudes brought to the New World from Spain concerning the individual's relation to space. According to Salvador de Madariaga, best known for his essay in comparative psychology, *Englishmen, Frenchmen, Spaniards,* the Spaniard thinks in universal *and* individual terms. The Spaniard founds his political system on the most universal element, religion, yet he sees things as extensions of himself or the individual self of others. Madariaga can say, then, that "...in Spain, liberty, justice, and free trade matter less than the particular Smith or Jones who is to incarnate them for the time being..." (Madariaga 32). In other words, as we have seen, the Spaniards brought with them to the New World the need for a *caudillo*—a particular Smith or Jones—who could incarnate values.

With such an egocentric, and yet universal, *weltanschauung*, space becomes a function of the hero, the individual self, the knight errant. In *Aquila Solitaria,* the hero subsumes space by being able to move— in the turn of a page—from one distant part of the world to another. He moves from the Mississippi to Salmon country in the Northwest to Navajo country in the Southwest to wherever. He dominates space, freeing it from geographical facts. The world becomes the individual.

Since Aquila Solitaria is in absolute control of himself and in absolute accord with community values, he can impose his values and his order within the space he dominates. The universal becomes the individual and the individual becomes the universe. According to Madariaga, such a concept of the individual came to Latin America as part of its Spanish heritage. He argues: "The individual...becomes the standard of all life...This individualist is an egoist. His person is the channel through which the life stream is made to pass, thus acquiring a personality polarized along a definite individual direction. The Spaniard therefore feels patriotism as he feels love—in the form of a passion whereby he absorbs the object of his love and assimilates it; that is to say, makes it his own. He does not belong to his country so much as his country belongs to him..." (31).

Since he controls himself and, as hero, in spite of many perilous adventures, controls his own destiny, Aquila Solitaria can incarnate the benevolent *caudillo* who must establish order on frontier space. Aquila Solitaria not only embodies the laws of his land, he *is* the law of his land. He repeats, over and over again, the primary law of his race, "To kill or be killed" (26,17 and 28,15 and on innumerable other pages). (Note: The first number in parenthetical references to *Aquila Solitaria* will be to the issue; the second number will be to the page in that issue). Aquila Solitaria knows all of the other laws of his race and as judge and juror measures the behavior of others as to their worthiness as Native Americans, as citizens of *his* country. If they attack from ambush they are not worthy. If they are cowards or if they succumb to torture they are not worthy, and so forth and so on. He embodies his racial mores— as defined by the comic book—and thereby his nation. He is therefore the absolute egoist and the absolute individualist, both absolutely necessary characteristics for a *caudillo*.

Aquila Solitaria sustains other traditional frontier motifs. As in *El cacique,* intruders on the frontier in *Aquila Solitaria* are savage and barbaric. On one occasion, Aquila Solitaria has an adventure with Gypsies. Gypsies were feared on the frontiers of Spain. From very early accounts of Gypsies in Western Europe, they were known to live nomadic lives—to have no respect for boundaries—and to have little respect for European concepts of honesty and property. From the beginning of the seventeenth century Gypsies were often charged with kidnapping children. Victims of racial prejudice, Gypsies were considered barbaric and thought to enslave those they captured.

When captured by a Gypsy hunting animals for his traveling circus, Aquila Solitaria is placed in a cage on wheels and put on exhibition. His captor refers to the hero as an animal (36,3,4,5,6). Aquila Solitaria, his captor says by way of advertising his circus, was caught while eating a Christian (36). All Native Americans, the Gypsy says, should be treated like beasts. A Gypsy woman, the wife of Aquila Solitaria's captor, wants to know if his people make love like animals (37,22). Aquila Solitaria, of course, escapes and then, by way of retaliation against her husband, shows the wife of his captor how he makes love.

According to old stories prevalent among the conquistadors, Amazons populated the far reaches of the world. California was discovered by a conquistador who was convinced he would find tribes of Amazons in the far West. Amazons were thought to dominate and enslave men.

No doubt the stories had some appeal as sexual fantasy for men who were traveling, for the most part, without women. The legend of a frontier populated by Amazons lives on in *Aquila Solitaria*. On various occasions, women warriors attack and imprison Aquila Solitaria. Such imprisonment and domination by a woman inevitably leads, in the comic books, to a crescendo of affirmation of the dominance of the male role in relationships. On one such occasion he tells Tania, an Amazon Queen who wears a black (perhaps leather?) mini-skirt and brassiere and keeps her warriors in line with a whip, that "When a woman loves a man, she learns to respect and obey the man. It is the law of my race" (43,16). He remarks when he sees one group of Amazons, "Women warriors, how absurd" (43,26). Of course Aquila Solitaria escapes their clutches. Finally, Aquila Solitaria kisses Tania, the woman likes it, and Toky, Aquila Solitaria's eagle friend, observes and knows that his owner has dominated—and possessed—the enemy (79,21).

Aquila Solitaria, set in the West of the United States, not only uses legends and folk knowledge from Spain, but also events and traditions from Latin American history and narrative, transposed to the United States, in order to communicate a vision of the frontier that is culturally Latin American. Pirates, their ship anchored on the Mississippi, take

Illustration Six: On yet another Amazonian adventure, when Aquila Solitaria finally catches his adversary, she struggles and says she will never be conquered by a man. He responds: "But I know how to dominate savages" (79,20) and in the next frame, "And to tame savage colts like you." "You will have to kill me," the woman responds (79,20).

slaves in one episode. The pirates would appear to have sprung from the seventeenth and eighteenth centuries. Captain Morgan, the head of the pirates, was, historically, a seventeenth-century Welsh buccaneer who ravaged the Spanish colonies in the Caribbean, eventually forcing the Spanish king to acknowledge Britain's title to Jamaica. Morgan attacked ports, stole Spanish gold, and as a consequence of his piratical behavior, the English made him acting governor of Jamaica. He was scarcely a friend or hero to the Spanish. In *Aquila Solitaria* he commands a slave ship, capturing Native Americans from North America as slaves, evidently to be sold wherever there might be a market. Since the terrain is definitely the far West of the United States, Captain Morgan's slave ship is in the wrong space and time. Pirates belong to the frontier tradition of Latin America. By the time Anglo America was being conquered, in the nineteenth-century, pirates such as Captain Morgan existed only in boy's adventure stories.

In yet another adventure, Native Americans are enslaved by mine owners. This was not, probably, peculiar to Latin America, but it is a form of racial relations more prevalent in sixteenth and seventeenth-century Latin America than in nineteenth-century Anglo America, where most mines were worked by the miners themselves with only casual help from indigenous people.

As was noted in the first chapter, many Spanish frontiersmen considered indigenous Americans to be without souls and therefore beasts, subject to domination and exploitation. The issue formed the basis for the crucial debates, mentioned earlier, between Bartolomé de las Casas and Juan Gines de Sepúlveda concerning the question of the humanity of Native Americans. The issue becomes a motif concerning racial relations throughout *Aquila Solitaria*. The Gypsies raise the question of Aquila Solitaria's humanity. During the pirate episode a pirate tells a Native American: "You dare to disrespect me, you who are only a savage animal of the prairies" (50,26). And on another occasion a pirate says of the captive Native Americans: "They are like savage animals. They do not have souls. Ha, Ha, Ha!" (51,5). As Captain Morgan prepares to rape Shiú, Aquila Solitaria's wife, the pirate remarks, "Although Indians do not have feelings, because they are like animals, I will divert myself with her" (51,8). During yet another adventure, when White Fox, an Apache chief, complains to the white soldier that he is not receiving compassionate treatment as a prisoner, the soldier responds, "One cannot have compassion for you Indians who are savage animals" (70,17).

The soldier's attitude toward Native Americans, and, many readers probably feel, toward Latin Americans as well, prevails among all Anglo Americans in the series. Perhaps because Spain suffered for nearly eight hundred years the presence of Moorish invaders, *Aquila Solitaria* promotes and reinforces images of barbaric behavior by intruders; however, in *Aquila Solitaria* the intruders are usually Anglo Americans. In one adventure a Calvary regiment imprisons Aquila Solitaria. The Calvary captain hates Aquila Solitaria for having humiliated him and abuses the hero without mercy (21). Indeed, on repeated occasions the Native Americans must fight the army of the United States (21,31/32; 23) and the army treats them brutally in prison (26). On other occasions they are hunted by Anglo Americans (26,19). Now and then the Anglo Americans try to starve them into submission (26,19). The Native Americans must also fight intruding Buffalo hunters (21), *Caras Palidas* (white faces), who attack them and call Aquila Solitaria an Indian dog (18). The brutality of the invading *Caras Palidas* seems to know no end. They hang Aquila Solitaria and others of the tribe upside down. In one episode Aquila Solitaria is tied to two horses that attempt to pull him apart (18).

During the pirate episode Aquila Solitaria discovers that his wife's village has been overrun by pirates and the young men and women taken prisoner. He says, obviously concerned, "I know the *Cara Palida* and I know how they treat my race" (49,15). When attacked by a pirate, Aquila Solitaria remarks, "You must be *Cara Palida* to attack from the back" (50,3). Aquila Solitaria counsels his eagle friend, Toky: "Remember that you must never have faith in the *Cara Palida*" (50,11). After freeing his fellow Native Americans from the pirates, Aquila Solitaria counsels them: "Don't ever forget that the *Cara Palida* is our eternal enemy" (55,23).

Racial stereotypes do not simply involve Anglo and Native Americans. In one, somewhat abbreviated episode, concerning the cruel behavior of a slave owner from the South, Aquila Solitaria helps a black woman, Bony. She warns Aquila Solitaria that the *Cara Palida* will enslave him "Because of his skin color" (56,18). Aquila Solitaria fights a battle with her lover, a huge, rebellious slave, but his primary battles are with the slave owner. He manages to escape, but Bony the black woman chooses to remain a slave. The implication seems to be that Blacks may well have brought their enslaved condition upon themselves.

Whatever the attitude communicated toward other races, in *Aquila Solitaria, Caras Palidas* are beneath contempt. They are cruel racists without regard for the lives of people of a different color. When Aquila Solitaria tries to leave the slave ranch he must knock down a cowboy who tries to stop him from taking Pinto, his faithful horse companion, but then he is held under gun by another cowboy. The other cowboy says, "No Negro, or Indian, has the right to even look at a White Man. We are the owners" (58,2).

Examples abound, but, above all, it was a representative of the Anglo world who caused Aquila Solitaria's life to become a troublesome adventure story worthy of a comic book series. Rocky Morgan, a villainous white man, killed Aquila Solitaria's parents when Aquila Solitaria was just a boy. Happily, a group of benevolent eagles picked the boy up and raised him in their nest. Of course they fitted him out with feathers and wings and taught him how to fly. Once grown he set out to avenge the murder of his parents. His quest is to find Rocky Morgan and kill him after punishing him in a suitable fashion. According to repeated assertions by Aquila Solitaria, all *Caras Palidas* are the same, stupid traitors at best, and no better than Rocky Morgan.

Although, to be sure, a very few Anglo Americans, such as Buffalo Bill, are depicted as honorable men, *Aquila Solitaria* promotes an image of the *Cara Palida* as a brutal intruder, and thus promotes a racist attitude toward the Anglo American as a brutal, uncivilized human being.

Illustration Seven: On an occasion when Aquila Solitaria is imprisoned by the white man's army, an army officer, after having beaten Aquila Solitaria when the noble hero was captive and helpless, tells him, "I am superior to you, because I am a white man" (71,15).

As in *El cacique*, the *caudillo* in *Aquila Solitaria* possesses enormous sexual prowess. He sexually possesses all the women he decides to possess. Anglo American women such as the Gypsy woman (who is referred to as a *Cara Palida)* like to be dominated and, since they tend to be sexually promiscuous, eagerly offer themselves to Aquila Solitaria (36,30). Queen Tania, the scantily clad Anglo American cowgirl, an Amazon, who rules a group of wretched men made subject by her witchcraft, as well as a domain of Amazonian women, takes the injured Aquila Solitaria to her camp and nurses his injuries suffered during a prior adventure. However, her motives are not pure. Like most Anglo American women—according to *Aquila Solitaria*—she is attracted by the hero's good looks and handsome body. However, when she tries to seduce Aquila Solitaria, he rejects her because she is a *Cara Palida* (47,24).

Such stories as *Aquila Solitaria* teach readers how to think about experience. His adventure filled world, free from the rules of adult reality, yet ironically a place where those rules, acted out in elaborate and highly

Illustration Eight: Later, as Aquila Solitaria, hanging upside down, protests to his soldier captor: "I don't need your compassion, *Cara Palida*. I only want to fight with you man to man." The soldier replies: "A red skin does not merit the honor of fighting with a white man" (71,24).

artificial episodes, becomes a place to inculcate guidelines for adult life. Ostensibly existing outside society, such stories—like games—serve as a means for socialization. The primary rules of the comic book series that bears his name teaches readers that a hero such as Aquila Solitaria must rule and possess and establish order on the frontier. In that way *Aquila Solitaria* sustains a primary tenet of *caudillaje*.

As in many games, the rules in *Aquila Solitaria* are articulated in a set of abstract cliches. Aquila Solitaria always demands to fight man to man. He frequently appeals to a code of honor which all good men follow—which is to say, all good Native Americans and a scant few good Anglo Americans (36,16). Aquila Solitaria never fights as a mercenary, (40,12) and thus does not want to fight for Tania, the Amazonian cowgirl queen, yet he can never forget that Tania saved his life (40,9). And, of course, according to Aquila Solitaria, "No one who has ever called me a coward has lived to tell of it" (41,31). The timeless, abstract rules of the game reflect the timeless, abstract rules of literary romance. Romance inculcates abstract morality, just as the rules of children's games require abstractions as characters, either as hero, princess, villain or evil queen. Acceptable and desirable adult roles are

Illustrations Nine and Ten. Aquila Solitaria is not a Christian (although on one occasion he reasons that the Anglo American's God may be very like his own deity). He certainly cannot share the ways of the 'savage' Native Americans who worship bears (4,9) and/ or those who eat human flesh (10,21).

reinforced by means of games—either in the form of stories, such as *Aquila Solitaria,* or in the form of games wherein cowboys shoot Indians by shouting at them and pointing a toy gun or an index finger.

Thus the good guys in *Aquila Solitaria* all live by highly social rules. Buffalo Bill, one of the few good Anglo Americans in the narrative, after having stopped an army officer from shooting Aquila Solitaria in the back, says, "A man should not be killed from behind," and, when the officer objects, Buffalo Bill says, "this Indian saved my life and I have a debt of honor with him." The officer, obviously a bad man, responds: "To the devil with honor. He is a criminal who merits punishment" (92,18,19). But Buffalo Bill prevails and Aquila Solitaria escapes. Nevertheless, with a true sense of honor toward the Army, just as Aquila Solitaria agreed with the Native Americans to bring Buffalo Bill in as a trade for Shiú and Kei, his wife and son, so Buffalo Bill makes an agreement with the army captain to bring Aquila Solitaria in for justice before the law of the *Caras Palidas* (92,21). The heroes all live by abstract codes, very close to fantasy, which define the rules of the game. The game, like romance, has no ending. The villains don't operate by the rules and constantly threaten the game with an end.

Machismo, emphasizing masculine dominance, violence, and a defiant attitude toward death, forms an important element in many Latin American societies. Boys learn to express male dominance through their play, and act such dominance out in their relationships with girls at school as well as at home. At least one observer has noted among Latin American young people a fascination with instruments of death, the machete among lower classes and guns among upper classes (Anderson 253). *Aquila Solitaria* reinforces *machismo.* The Native American hero repeats, over and over again, the law of his race, "To kill or to die," often enough to make it clear that he has absolutely no fear of death. Indeed, he says exactly that on many occasions, and challenges his enemies to kill him when he is a captive, lest when he is free he take vengeance upon them.

Aquila Solitaria takes considerable pains to prove that he can defy death. He takes as many pains to prove male dominance. He is in absolute charge of his family. He orders Shiú, his wife, to go to the village of her parents when he has some hero's work to do. Even though they have been separated for many moons, Shiú goes and promises to wait forever, presumably as a faithful wife (34,15). As a good wife, Shiú understands perfectly what Aquila Solitaria must teach Tania, that "When a woman loves a man, she learns to respect and obey the man. It is the law of my race" (43,16). Aquila Solitaria must also instruct other women concerning their roles—which are distinctly different from those of the warrior hero. One Amazonian tribe attacks him, but Aquila Solitaria escapes and determines to teach them a lesson. "Women should attend the home fires. Weapons are for men," he tells them (44,6). When an Amazon captures him and hangs him by his hands from a tree, he lectures her anyway, "You will never be a warrior because you are a traitorous woman" (44,20).

Aquila Solitaria finds it an attractive idea to remain faithful to Shiú, his wife, and occasionally thinks of his only "clean and true love" (48,10). But a hero's work requires all kinds of sacrifice, and although he must be faithful to many rules of the game, fidelity to his wife is not one of those rules. He makes love to the Gypsy woman, a *Cara Palida* (37,29). Most women find him irresistible and that, evidently, makes it reasonable for him to share his favors. Tania, saved by Aquila Solitaria from the Devil, can't help but give herself to him (41,13;43,18).

Anglo American women, especially ready to offer themselves to the handsome man, intrigue Aquila Solitaria. Such dalliance receives tacit approval in the games Aquila Solitaria plays. Shortly after defeating the pirates on the Mississippi river, he is attracted by the Anglo American girl, the fiancé of Kent, the foreman of a railroad crew somewhere in the far West. "She is as light as a feather, her skin is white and smooth, like a pigeon," Aquila Solitaria notes (104,10). He thinks of her later: "Her eyes appear like the sky and her mouth is as red as blood" (104,14). After saving her life twice, Aquila Solitaria and the lovely *Cara Palida* engage in what appears to be foreplay (105,12). Yet another Anglo American girl, a miner crazed by gold fever, offers herself to Aquila Solitaria in a cave during a snowstorm (130,30). After Aquila Solitaria has started down the mountain, letting the girl go on toward a cave of gold in the middle of the winter—and thus toward certain death— he recalls the night before, when "Even her lips had the sweet taste of the kisses of a white woman" (131,10). Ruby, yet another Anglo American woman with rather loose morals, shares body warmth with Aquila Solitaria during his adventures with Crazy Horse (156,2). But no matter how many *Caras Palidas* fall in love with him, and how interesting he finds them for the moment, Aquila Solitaria always tells them, "Our roads soon will part forever. You are a white woman and I am a Red Skin" (156,4). Nevertheless, like other *caciques*, Aquila Solitaria can possess all women who happen to come within his dominion.

Anglo American women are attracted to Aquila Solitaria, but he is often distracted by lovely women of his own race as well. The rules for being a man, the comic argues, require considerable sexual energy. One episode in particular illustrates Aquila Solitaria's plight as a husband and father who, throughout the story, rides whenever he can toward his hidden valley refuge where his wife and child await him, but who simply can't pass up an adventure. Once he is captured by an Amazon tribe living in trees. The tribe of Amazons began to live in trees after they were attacked by Anglo Americans. Only one warrior (now old) and his wife (now dead) escaped the attack and took up life in the trees in order to survive. Unhappily, the old chief's wife only brought forth girls, and none of them marry since they never leave the trees where they live and therefore never find husbands. In fact, the girls of the tree tribe do not even know what love is, but their father assures them that their captive, Aquila Solitaria, will teach them (76,8). However, male pride and a momentary fit of fidelity trouble the hero. For a frame or two he is given to thoughts of Shiú and his responsibilities as a husband (76,12). But then he recalls the fact that he has been *ordered* to make love to all the lovely young girls. His macho spirit offended by the inversion of male and female roles, he escapes and vows to teach the tree women a lesson because, "A woman should never carry arms against a man" (77,10).

Yet, Aquila Solitaria is able to temper justice with mercy. The old man, the chief of the Amazon ladies of the trees, begs Aquila Solitaria to make love to his beautiful daughters: "At least may you make the ritual of love with them [his daughters] and thus they will have children. It will be our salvation," (77-30) the old man pleads. Aquila Solitaria asks him: "How can you be sure that they will give you male children?" The old man replies: "You are strong and vigorous like a puma. Your blood will give warrior descendants and my tribe will survive" (77,30).

Aquila Solitaria looks at the lovely girls and finally says: "Good. I accept. I will be the husband of your daughters in order to create descendants" (77,32). Under such duress, Aquila Solitaria tells the daughters: "I will choose one of you and thus it will be each night" (78,15). He chooses one, then orders the others away. Tenderly he prepares to make love, reassuring the young virgin: "You will discover that love is not a condemnation but an incomparable happiness" (78,18). But just as Aquila Solitaria is about to sacrifice himself for the greater good of the community, the older sister, who has tried to kill Aquila Solitaria against her father's will, shoots an arrow at him, misses, and kills her younger sister, the first initiate. Although the older sister gets in the way for various frames, Aquila Solitaria eventually does his duty by the tribe. It takes him two weeks.

On various occasions Shiú, Aquila Solitaria's wife, finds herself nearly at the mercy of a pirate or Rocky Morgan or even a member of her own race who believes Aquila Solitaria to be dead. However, in the nick of time, she always manages to remain chaste in anticipation of her husband's return.

The comic book audience evidently shares with other Latin American audiences considered herein a sense of the frontier as a fearful place where the strong man has the responsibility to impose order on those about him. The order is, however, entirely personal; it exists within

Illustration Eleven. "Two weeks have passed
since Aquila Solitaria arrived. The warrior
has already completed his sentence...."

the hero. One does not sense that the tribe living in the trees, even with
a new crop of male babies, will found a permanent and stable civilization.
As Aquila Solitaria moves on he takes with him the order and stability
he has established. He saves his own life and the lives of others who
deserve to be saved, he helps villages escape immediate danger, but he
does not create a permanent order divorced from himself.

For this reason Aquila Solitaria has much more in common with
a *caudillo* or, since his domain usually does not encompass a large
population, a *cacique,* than with a frontiersman from the United States,
who establishes order on the frontier and then moves on to new frontiers,
leaving stable settlements behind. Aquila Solitaria can scarcely be seen
as the forerunner for an expanding, intruding population, i.e. a hero
such as Daniel Boone, Hawkeye, Buffalo Bill, or Roy Rogers. He can
provide order and justice within communities with which he comes into
contact. He thus illustrates the necessity within those communities for
a strong man who can impose order, i.e. a *cacique. Aquila Solitaria*
illustrates how cultural attitudes made evident by historical events and

narratives from the cultural past continue to dominate frontier ideology in popular media in Latin America.

Rius: The Caudillo *and Anglo America*

Rius (the pen name of Eduardo del Río) writes comic books for a sophisticated, and no doubt highly educated, audience. His comics, internationally acclaimed, are characterized by political satire, the absence of a strong story line, lengthy expository passages substantiated by statistical evidence, footnotes, and a bibliography. If all that makes them sound dull then Rius has been done a disservice. His wicked sense of the satirical makes his comic book histories good reading, with or without total assent with his political views.

Rius, like other serious artists to be examined later, uses his art to criticize Latin American dependence upon *caudillaje*. Yet, like *El cacique* and *Aquila Solitaria*, his works reflect some traditional attitudes toward the frontier and, in the process of his critical examination of *caudillaje*, he demonstrates how pervasive those attitudes are, even among his educated audience. His contemporary frontier stories, like the stories of the *cacique* and *Aquila Solitaria*, present a view of the frontier as savage. He warns readers of the dangers of venturing too far from centers of their own culture, and especially of venturing into the wilderness of Anglo American life. Therefore, like the popular image literature previously considered, his comics promote the implosive myth of the frontier characteristic of Latin America.

Probably Rius' most famous works are the two series: *Los supermachos [The Supermales]* and *Los agachados [The Crouching Ones]*. He treats the problem of frontiers in at least two numbers of *Los agachados*: Number 173, October 16, 1974, *"Otra industria sin chimeneas: Los braceros"* ["Another Industry Without Chimneys: The Mexican Worker in the United States"] and in Number 248, March, 1976, *"Viven más gringos en mexico que braceros en ee.uu."* ["More Anglo Americans live in Mexico than Mexican Workers in the United States"].

In the comic but scholarly world of Rius, the frontiersman crosses a frontier purely for monetary gain and, usually after suffering greatly or inflicting great suffering upon others, loses his soul. In the 1974 work, *"Los braceros,"* Rius introduces us to an immigrant worker returning to his village after a stay in the United States.

Visual signs immediately tell us of the worker's degeneracy. He is wearing an outrageous, tourist-style shirt, and, in the world of Rius, tourists are associated with degenerate behavior. This frontiersman's hair is long and red—perhaps dyed in an effort to appear blond—and his trousers are 'bell bottomed' (quite stylish in the United States in 1974, as well as in Mexico, but scarcely appropriate for a village person). His

Illustration Twelve: *Los agachados,* Number 173

manner of walking, along with other visual signs which follow, suggest that he has become effeminate while among the people of the United States. His hat is odd. Its vegetation motif and unusual shape suggest, perhaps, a vestigial pre-Columbian side to the man's nature, which not even his experiences across the frontier could eradicate. Rius, after all, would like to see all Mexicans identified, in one way or another, with Native Americans.

The first frame of the comic shows us a close-up of the frontiersman. He affects pink-rimmed dark glasses and speaks with a musical lilt as he announces his return. The inhabitants of the village bar are offended by his manner. They think he is, at best, a foreigner. One customer of the bar suggests that he might be a politician traveling incognito, which is to say, perhaps more depraved than a tourist, but the older man assumes the very worst—that the stranger is a spy sent by the Central Intelligence Agency (spelled and pronounced as *chia,* for C.I.A., by the village people).

Illustration Thirteen: *Los agachados*, Number 173

Illustration Fourteen: *Los agachados*, Number 173 "Incognito,
you say. To me he looks more like a spy from the C.I.A."
"Well, I don't think so. More likely I would say that....Son
of a bitch but he looks like Acocil Diaz!"

Illustration Fifteen: *Los Agachados,* Number 173

Although the two village men in the bar see something about the *bracero* as familiar, and even identify him with a local family name, he is no longer 'one of them.' He has been made strange by his experience among strangers; the village is not his home. The returning immigrant's language, as well as other cultural characteristics, have been contaminated through contact with Anglo Americans. In one frame, not included, he drops into song in English, and when he speaks he uses a very bad mixture of Spanish and English, so bad it is scarcely worthy of the label of dialect.

"Yes men," he says in English and then switches to Spanish (more or less) to ask, "How can I help you, yeah?" (*Yeah* is phonetically in Spanish, but obviously an English word.) He does not wait for an answer, but aggressively continues, presumptuously thinking that the village people will want something from him, and, moreover, that they share his materialistic and debased concerns. He asks if they would like him to get them some wash and wear shirts, pornographic pictures, contraband cigarettes, and in frames not included as illustrations, false immigration papers and contraband electrical appliances. The two village men want none of such stuff, but they do want to identify him within the world of the village. When they press him concerning his identity he replies in a garble of English and Spanish that requires considerable attention and knowledge of both languages to understand, a level of language sophistication which Rius assumes his readers will have.

"Esquiusmii," [*excuse me,* more or less rendered in Spanish]

"Ostedes" [a deformed version of *Ustedes*] "confundirrme" [*mistake me,* but one must notice the hard *r* sound suggested by the doubling of the consonant in *confundirrme*. English speakers have difficulty with the trilled *r* in Spanish, so it often sounds like a long nasal *r* rather than trilled. The frontiersman who has had prolonged contact with Anglo Americans cannot pronounce a basic sound in Spanish.] "Mi serr Francis Days." This is somewhat grammatically equivalent to saying in English, "My be Francis Days."

When a sober village elder, Don Céfiro, correctly identifies the return immigrant as a former villager, the prodigal observes: "Oh my God!" in English, then switches to Spanish to continue, "Now I'm leaving! They mistake me here for one of these stupid village hicks." Francis Days, the return immigrant, functions as a satiric example of the effects of life across the border in the United States on the dignity and culture of a Mexican. Don Céfiro, educated and firmly a part of his village culture, passes judgment for the village: "That's how it is," he notes. "They no more than leave the village and when they return they are unbearable."

In verbal and pictorial form, the rest of the issue consists of a lecture—presumably with Don Céfiro as the spokesman for the community—on the problems of the Mexican worker in the United States. The problem began, Don Céfiro tells us, when the United States crossed the frontier

Illustration Sixteen: *Los agachados,* Number 173

Illustration Seventeen: *Los agachados,* Number 173

into Mexico's northern territory—now the states of most of the Western United States—an action which, as the Rius reader knows, ultimately led to the acquisition by the United States of nearly half of Mexico's territory. Don Céfiro tells us in his lecture (accompanied by witty visual aids), that many Mexican farmers were forced to become frontiersmen, to strike out from their homes in search of subsistence among Anglo Americans. They usually found only misery and poverty, serving in the most menial ways and living in miserable ghettos.

Their pride and identity gone, they try to hide their nationality through Americanization, changing their names as they change their language. Modern Mexican frontier people, as presented by Rius, can scarcely be seen as in any way equivalent to the Sacketts of L'Amour's many printed novels. Instead they are to be pitied, forced to live in an alien and savage world as virtual slaves to a racist society.

It must be noted that Rius' editorial position does not always coincide with experience. It fails to do justice to those many millions of Americans from Mexico who have forged good lives in the United States, even if they, like many other immigrant groups, no longer speak the language of their ancestors nor remember all of their ancestral customs. Rius does not say anything about the many Latin Americans who have been successful in the United States.

In Number 248 of *Los agachados,* published in March of 1976, Rius argued that *"Viven más gringos en mexico que braceros en ee.uu."* ["More

Illustration Eighteen: *Los agachados,* Number 173 "Oh no," Roberto Enaguas protests: "My name is Bob Petticoat," since *enaguas* means petticoat in Spanish. In the same illustration on the right Pedro Estrella tells us, in poorly pronounced English, "Mi name es Peter Star, Plis!" Peter Star's baby, ironically, in good Spanish, reveals that his name has been completely Americanized—as Billy.

Anglo Americans live in Mexico than Mexican workers in the United States"]. In this issue Rius treats the problem of Anglo immigrants in Mexico, which he perceives as a serious threat to Mexican autonomy and culture. Such frontiersman, as Rius presents them, were either degraded before crossing the frontier into Mexico, or were degraded by the experience of living outside their own culture. As in the previous comic considered, the moral is quite clear; frontier life defiles.

Rius appears to accept a conspiracy theory as an explanation for the phenomenon. He depicts representatives of the United States government, such as the Central Intelligence Agency, in collusion with transnational business interests, actively conspiring to invade Mexico.

But Rius is not content with simply describing the United States' invasion of Mexico; he seeks to provide an explanation for the explosive Anglo American frontier behavior. His answer, however, is rather vague. Simply referring the cause for an expansionist frontier policy to "economic and sociological necessities," without detailing what those necessities are, scarcely tells why such a policy has prevailed throughout the history of the United States.

Nevertheless, Rius presents a vision of the frontiersman as helpless

Illustration Nineteen: *Los agachados*, Number 248 "Aside from Canada," the narrator observes, "Mexico has the largest collection of trashy North Americans (war crazed veterans, drug addicts, hippies, old and decrepit people, C.I.A. agents, executives and so forth) of all the Third World countries." Worse yet, these modern frontiersmen, the balloon commentary indicates, are often "directly involved in the economic and political life of the country."

victim or degenerate outcast, which does help to explain the history of Latin America's frontier behavior. Such ideas scarcely urge venturing individuals to seek new worlds to conquer, and obviously Rius and his readers see intruders—especially those from their northern frontier—as a threat to their economic and social well being. Rius and his readers evidently feel that Mexico's northern frontier should not be crossed, either coming or going. Although Rius would never support *caudillaje*, and indeed we will see later how he critically examines the phenomenon, the fear of frontiers he fosters in the two comics examined above ratify traditional community values and the need for traditional order. *Caudillos* often call upon tradition and the need for order to obtain and sustain their power.

Rius' defensive posture toward the frontier between Mexico and the United States, and indeed between the United States and all of Latin America, is underscored in *Los Dictaduros: El Militarismo en America Latina [The Dictators: Militarism in Latin America]*, in which he seeks a historical explanation for the predominance of military *caudillos* in Latin America since the arrival of the Spanish. Rius takes the moral high ground assumed by many Latin American intellectuals—that of the Nobel Savage—of the pre-Columbian Native American whose innocence was violated by invaders from Europe, and whose rights have

Illustration Twenty: *Los agachados,* Number 248 Rius lectures in the legend at the top of illustration twenty: "Just like the cowboys did during the conquest of the West, when they invaded lands which did not belong to them and later rented the same land to the people who lived there first..." [and then in the balloon speaking from the sun] "So today's cowboys of capitalism have been given the job of conquering Mexico."

¿POR QUÉ LO HACEN? EN GRAN PARTE
PROBABLEMENTE TENGA QUE VER CON
LAS NECESIDADES ECONÓMICAS Y
SOCIOLÓGICAS DE LA GRAN OLIGARQUÍA
GRINGA QUE SIEMPRE QUIERE MÁS Y MÁS
Y MÁS ...

¡BAH!
SI HEMOS
PERDIDO VIETNAM
CUBA Y OTROS
PAÍSES, TODAVÍA
PODEMOS TENER
CHILE, MÉXICO
Y OTROS MÁS.

Illustration Twenty One: *Los agachados,* Number 248 "Why do they do it?" the narrator
asks, and answers: "For the most part it probably has to do with economic and sociological
necessities of the great *gringa* oligarchy which always wants more and more and more..."
"Bah," Uncle Sam remarks in the balloon, clutching a fist full of buildings—presumably
Latin American real estate, "If we have lost Vietnam, Cuba and other countries, we still
have Chile, Mexico and many more."

been violated for generations by invaders from Europe and the United
States.

Rius' clever use of language equates the word of God with militarism,
and sexual intercourse with preaching Christianity and the gospel of
modern war making. Such intercourse—sexual and otherwise—eventually
convinces "the Indians of the superior goodness of militarism and converts
them into faithful vassals of their civilizers who generously deigned to
give them their blood with the nobel end of improving the race" (*Los
Dictaduros* 18). Rius' irony is possible because he has assumed as the
idea—against which the evil realities of militarism are depicted—the
stance of an innocent, passive Noble Savage tricked by the materialism
(note the gifts being brought to Cortéz in illustration twenty two) and
the lust of the Spaniards who invaded their frontiers.

As in his other comic book treatments of the frontier, Rius perceives
cultural domination—and penetration—equally as dangerous as military
domination. The man who crosses a frontier brings disorder and even
death.

Illustration Twenty Two: *Los Dictaduros,* 10 "Those glorious soldiers," he tells us in the legend on the left of illustration twenty two, "brought us [the Native Americans] military knowledge, not only theoretical but practical, based on the noble principle that the word [of God] will enter with blood [through interbreeding]," "teaching us in a practical way the technology of firearms and how to make bullets. (They also brought us faith, hope and charity, all free...)" And in the balloon the conquistador assures the prostrate Native American, "Have faith! This won't hurt in the least."

In illustration twenty three, in which the old pistol is pointed at the head of the Native American working in the mine (and one must recall the millions of indigenous people who gave their lives in the Spanish mines), Rius tells us: "We must also note the enormous contribution of the military to the education of the aborigines in the methods of work and the adoption of discipline and responsibility, so necessary in order to achieve progress. They said, even before the great Adolph, that *Arbeit macht frei,* or something like that." The balloon translates the German: "Work shall make us free." People who intrude, such as the Spaniards, bring debased foreign values and enslave peaceful natives.

The peaceful natives were not freed by the nineteenth-century wars of independence. As Rius explains in illustration twenty four, nineteenth-century Latin American revolutions were dominated by the aristocratic Creole class, i.e. the landed gentry born in the New World who,

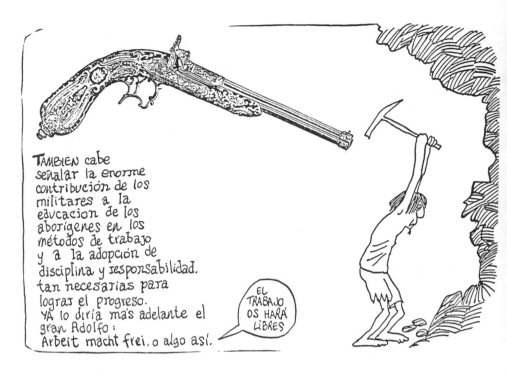

Illustration Twenty Three: *Los Dictaduros,* 22

nevertheless, as long as their countries were but colonies of Spain, could never achieve total power. However, from the point of view of the Native American whose territory had been invaded by the Spaniards, the revolution simply substituted the Creole aristocracy for the Spanish crown; the economic and social plight of the exploited class did not change.

But the new governors, however rich, did not have experience in affairs of state. They needed teachers, and (see illustration twenty five), the great powers of Europe, England, Germany, and France, were most willing to fulfill that need. "The first lesson," the balloon in the left center counsels, "is how to maintain order." To have the nightsticks and the horsemen necessary to maintain order, "It was necessary therefore to professionalize the armed forces in order to duly exercise power." The legend continues in the lower left corner: "And how can we pay for this favor?" the Latin American military *caudillo* asks. "Easy," replies his European adviser. "We don't even want money. Only concessions." Concessions, of course, refer to the practice of many Latin American *caudillos* of granting mineral, railroad, port, and factory rights (an entire

Illustration Twenty Four: *Los Dictaduros*, 33

Illustration Twenty Five: *Los Dictaduros*, 39

sea in Gabriel Garcia Márquez' novel, *El Otoño del Patriarca)* in exchange for capital. The practice led to the continued rape of the Edenic (at least according to the myth) world of the Latin American by foreign powers.

Rius then traces the careers of military *caudillos* throughout Latin America's long history, but he pays special attention to those who were most disposed to sell their nation's rights to foreign invaders, a group which contrasts with a few who nationalized their nation's wealth and shored up their frontiers in the service of social justice and human rights. Among those eager to sell out he gives several pages to Trujillo of the Dominican Republic, Solano López of nineteenth-century Paraguay, Stroessner of twentieth-century Paraguay, Juan Vicente Gómez of early twentieth-century Venezuela, along with, of course, Porfirio Diaz of Mexico and the Somoza family of Nicaragua. Among the nationalistic *caudillos* with a social conscience—a much smaller group—he includes Jacobo Arbenz of Guatemala, deposed, according to Rius, by the United States, Perón of Argentina, deposed, again, according to Rius, by Argentine military men with the blessing of the Pentagon and the Vatican, Lázaro Cárdenas of Mexico, who dared to defy the United States by nationalizing his country's oil, and Torrijos of Panama, who dared to demand from the United States Panama's right to the Canal. Good *caudillos,* in Rius comics, are those who are willing to confront the power of the United States in the effort to make their national resources serve the people of their nations.

Such, he argues, is history's lesson for Latin America. After the European powers were weakened by World War I, the United States began its expansion into the entire hemisphere (having begun in Mexico during the early years of the nineteenth-century). Theodore Roosevelt (see illustration twenty six), according to Rius' version of history, recognized that the United States could take advantage of political unrest in Latin America without fomenting revolution. Rius labels the first Roosevelt president the "Inventor and great practitioner of the big stick, and putative grandfather of Mr. Reagan." Later, he argues, during the decade of the 1930s, when Latin Americans such as Cárdenas were nationalizing oil fields, the insistence of some countries to the right to exploit their own resources gave the United States some problems; however, World War II came along and military intervention by the United States could then be blamed on the necessity to defend the hemisphere against fascism.

In 1942 the Act of Chapultepec—a mutual defense pact for the hemisphere—was signed. It permitted the United States to use Latin American territory for radar installations and even troop deployment sites. This led to military training missions being sent to the area, which

Illustration Twenty Six: *Los Dictaduros.*

led to arms sales, and that led to loans to the countries to pay for the purchase of arms, and from that to debt, and dependency. As Rius sees history, during World War II the threat of foreign fascist intervention served to cow Latin Americans into submission to the United States; after World War II the threat of foreign communist intervention served the same end, as the United States maintained Latin American military governments in a dependent relationship with its own armed forces.

Moreover, the United States provided professional training for Latin American military men who, (see illustration twenty seven) taking their training home, established "Order, Discipline, National Unity, Development and National Security" which, we are told, meant "Zero democracy, zero strikes, zero nationalism, zero liberty and zero ideology" or, as the smirking general in the lower right says, "Home grown fascism, in a word, or two..." With such methods, eventually Brazil, Argentina, Uruguay, Bolivia, Chile, Paraguay, Peru, and Ecuador were dominated by military governments which, in turn, were dominated by the United States.

Arms sales, Rius contends, have been and continue to be a magnificent business for the United States (see illustration twenty eight). The bald general in the lower left corner notes that "No en balde...," [that it's not in vain] "that the true governors of the United States are the big companies that manufacture military arms." The 'centerpiece,' the same drawing used on the 'frontispiece' of the book, in its depiction of the penis as a canon, suggests the *machismo* which Rius sees as the psychological basis for militarism. On the right the legend explains: "If the sale of arms were interrupted, the United States would suffer economic chaos." The enlisted man explains in his balloons: "350,000 United States citizens would be without jobs, the Gross National Product would fall by 12 billion dollars and a whole bunch of generals would throw a fit."

The military *caudillos* of Latin America, according to Rius' version of history, feed from the hand of military power in the United States. "That's how it is, my boys," a reclining Uncle Sam assures the dogs of Latin American militarism surrounding him. "While I'm alive you're not going to do without anything."

But even though, as Rius sees it, the United States is a dying organism, having lost Nicaragua and is in the process of losing El Salvador, "...the empire is a cadaver which enjoys good health" and, as we see, is still devouring Latin America by means of transnational business with the help of the Central Intelligence Agency. As the legend on the right of the picture above tells us, "The death of the emperor (and father of

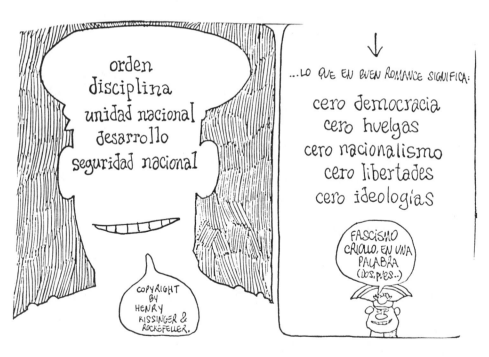

Illustration Twenty Seven: *Los Dictaduros,* 128

Illustration Twenty Eight: *Los Dictaduros,* 140

militarism) does not depend only on the wish—everyday more widespread—that such a death should occur. The problem is to correlate the strength, [to depose the emperor] not of desire [to do it]." The statement is reinforced by the worker figure in the lower right of the drawing who affirms, in strident rhetoric, the coming revolution: "It is the struggle of everyone, workers, intellectuals, priests, political parties, the people and the armed forces..."

For Rius, European—and later United States'—domination explains the prevalence of military *caudillos* in Latin America. Whether such is or is not the truth is not at issue here, but rather with the type of reader Rius appeals to and the frontier ideology those readers share, an ideology that is embedded far deeper in the culture than political and economic concepts such as capitalism and/or socialism.

Rius readers must, obviously, be literate in Spanish and familiar enough with English and the permeations of both languages in the speech of people who cross frontiers to be able to recognize, and enjoy, the numerous language games Rius likes to play. They must also share a sophisticated interest in history and historical explanations of social and political conditions. They must be willing to sacrifice narrative, exciting

Illustration Twenty Nine: *Los Dictaduros,* 157

Illustration Thirty: *Los Dictaduros,* 156

events, heroic and beautiful characters and exotic settings (standard fare in comic books for a less literate readership) for the sake of a highly abstract lecture, even though the graphics provide humorous and varied visual stimulation. Rius readers represent, in short, a large segment of the educated, intellectual class. If they buy and enjoy Rius, it is likely they have already accepted the version of history he communicates. That version proclaims the danger inherent in crossing a frontier and in allowing a frontier to be crossed. The stockade, as impenetrable in either direction as possible, projects Rius' concept of a frontier.

A pattern for seeing the frontier experience which appeals to widely different Latin America audiences clearly emerges from the film genre, the *Comedia Ranchera,* and the three different kinds of comics examined. A Rius audience represents one class of Latin American society. *Aquila Solitaria* probably appeals to a less erudite group of people, while *El cacique* most likely appeals to all kinds of people, although certainly those with advanced degrees only read such matter in the interest of popular culture scholarship. The *Comedia Ranchera* celebrates the stability and order of a past when *caudillos* ruled provincial worlds, when the lower class, the *peones* and *campesinos,* were quaint and grateful. The comics depict a less settled world. The narrators assume the point of view of the Native American, exploited and invaded in all ways. The readers evidently identify and sympathize with this point of view. Such a rhetorical stance would not appeal if the audience saw themselves as part of an invading people rather than as people whose land is under threat of invasion. In Rius' comics the invaders bring corruption, dependence, and degradation for the descendants of the Noble Savage. In the comics of Rius, those invaders are ultimately, after all the historical facts have been exposed, from the United States. In the pornographic work the outsider is simply an outsider, apparently Spanish. However, he exploits the village people by buying cheap and selling for more money, as well as by raping the wives of his employees. He is, above all, an intruder, and he brings social and moral disruption to the Edenic wilderness he possesses, evidently through the force of his personality. In the story of *Aquila Solitaria,* once again the Noble Savage must use natural strength and powers (Eagle training) to confront the technology and treachery of Anglo Americans in order to impose his personal order upon space. In all three comics intruding frontiersmen—most commonly from the United States—cause men to lose their culture, their forms for civilized sexual behavior, and, of course, quite often their lives. The best the indigenous people can do is to close the frontiers, to hide their loved ones from contact with invaders, and to put their faith in a strong individual who can maintain order.

It is scarcely strange that the Marxist-Leninists who assume the stance of the Noble Savage threatened by the treachery of the United States should have such success among many people in Latin America. Latin Americans are conditioned, partially by historical experience and partially by narratives told in omnipresent comics and films about life on frontiers, to shape new experience in accord with a pattern of thought that sees Anglo American international businessmen and politicians as intruders who threaten peaceful natives who wish only to be left alone.

Chapter VI
The Cowboy Defamiliarized:
Clark, Doctorow, Berger, and Shaefer

Topsy-Turvy:
The Ox-Bow Incident and Welcome to Hard Times

Popular narratives, such as *Aquila Solitaria,* the films of Gene Autry and *Comedias Rancheras,* the novels of Louis L'Amour and M.L. Estefanía, all tend toward perfect form which can be repeated over and over again. Serious artists see an imperfect world. Gene Autry's popular films and comics repeat plot, character, and incident and become extremely predictable, although their stylized narratives pretend to represent a historical past, the way the West of the United States was won by Anglo Americans—with the Cass County Boys following along in close harmony. Yet almost everyone, except for the most ardent fans, would acknowledge that Westerns, like the comics featuring Aquila Solitaria, present a world of play, with rules which require every game to be essentially the same. Serious writers, who do not want to simply play a well known game, often use that world of play in order to contrast their vision with the abstractions of popular narrative. Their *words,* in a sense, respond to the popular images which reduce discourse, analysis, and thought to automatic response.

Many writers parody popular narrative. Others enter into that world of play in order to explore what it means to the society that plays such games. Since serious artists use and explore the world of popular literature, the study of popular narratives of a well defined type, such as the Western, which presents simplified images in lieu of thought about the problems of frontiers, can lead to a more complete reading of serious works of literature which use, or abuse, popular narrative patterns and themes.

The narrative pattern called the Western, worn so smooth by popular authors, continues to attract viewers and readers. Although Western television series, such as "Bonanza," "Gunsmoke," and "Wyatt Earp," enormously popular in prime time during the 1960s, now serve only as time fillers for low budget television stations, Louis L'Amour's novels continue to sell in incredible numbers. Moreover, the pattern for the imagination inculcated by the Western has been translated from the cowboy trails and Native American battles of the nineteenth century to

109

twentieth century urban scenes where savage street fighters must be tamed by hard hitting, straight shooting, good guy detectives who make the cities safe for colonists and civilization.

The setting changes; the pattern remains the same. With the change in setting, contemporary social phenomenon can be introduced. The bad guy can be a cocaine dealer working for a gang lord instead of a hired gun working for a big rancher unwilling to allow homesteaders on his feudal range; the chase scene can take place through crowded slums, obviously made barren by the rule of savagery and in need of redemptive colonization, instead of across prairies left untended by savage Native Americans. A hero's white horse can easily become a private detective's sleek sport car. Sam Lundwall, in *Science Fiction: What It's All About,* argues that "if the Colt six-shooter were substituted for the space-age weapon, and if the Western frontier and its Indians took the place of the interplanetary frontiers and their manifold denizens, the 'space opera' would convert very simply into 'horse opera' " (Tucker 22). The story can move to future time as well as to present time.

In spite of temporal and spatial change, the worn narrative pattern continues to provide forms through which readers and viewers prefer to imagine the way their cultures should behave in the frontier paradigms, where two or more races or cultures collide. The durability of the patterns attest to their strength as determinates for national policies and personal behavior.

Nevertheless, stories about the West of the United States had scarcely begun to establish their conventions before they became subject to parody. The tall tales of the West, used by Twain, were parodic responses to the romantic, abstract visions of the West provided by popular narratives of the day. Western films had just established their enduring popularity when, in the early decades of this century, stars such as Mack Sennett and Douglas Fairbanks began to parody them for comic effect (Everson 61).

Parody strikes an agreement with the reader—or viewer—that the story being parodied lacks sufficient relationship with reality to be taken seriously. Through exaggeration, parody draws attention to the conventional elements of the original. Parody strikes at conventions and patterns which distort reality. Since conventions, or narrative patterns, embody the ideology of the readers entertained by such narratives, worn narratives not only appeal to serious writers who want to get a laugh by kidding a cliché, but also to serious artists who wish to examine the psychological or social or philosophical implications of the pattern in the narrative for those who use that pattern as a way of knowing.

People laughing at a parody of a Western are not simply laughing at the comedian's pratfalls from a horse. Complex and difficult as the topic may be, without oversimplification one may agree with Henri

Bergson, the turn of the century French philosopher who argued that, by overemphasizing spatial concepts, which suggest a fixed, static reality, people underestimate the power of time, in which everything constantly changes. Thus comedy and laughter often, if not always, grow from the encounter between rigidity of conventions—character, plot, incident, or idea—which lock those elements into patterns, fixed in the mind as if they were fixed in space and therefore incapable of change—and the fluid nature of reality in a world of time where things are constantly changing, a world perceived by those not caught up by the patterns enforced by popular ways. The parodist asks the reader to stand outside the story and laugh at the exaggerated behavior of the characters or the exaggerated descriptions of events and settings. The laughter stems from the knowledge that a rigid, formulaic plot—or setting or incident—predicates the exaggerated behavior and that the ludicrous fiction violates the fluid nature of reality.

It is perhaps rare that a parody does not make it explicit what characteristics of the original pattern are being held up to the light of laughter. Perhaps it would simply be impossible to create parody of something totally unfamiliar to an audience. However, an audience is not always aware of the social and political implications of the original, and thus not always completely conscious that the slapstick cowboy not only ridicules the character and plot of the overused form but also the *ideas* implicit in the overused form. The swaggering comedian swaggers *like* a cowboy, and thus makes himself, and the cowboy, the object of laughter. But for those who have bothered to think about it, the ideology the standardized film cowboy embodies becomes as funny as the cowboy who has fallen from his horse.

Parody is certainly not the only way a fictional pattern treating a specific theme, such as frontier life, may be explored by writers who see that a certain fiction, when repeated over and again, has cultural significance. Many serious writers attempt more subtle examinations of the implications of a popular narrative pattern by working from *within* the imagined world of highly conventionalized narrative. By doing so they ask their readers or viewers to perceive, while accepting the *as if* world of the fiction as truth, how characters and settings and events are affected by living in a world dominated by the rigidity of ideology and event and character that the parodist attacks.

Such serious work sometimes must assume a complete knowledge, not only of the form itself, but also of the implications, social and cultural, of the fictional pattern. Studies of the narrative patterns that embody the ideology of a community of believers in certain popular narratives can enhance readings of both parodic works based on those patterns as well as more subtle works which examine the culture of people who allow the ideology from popular images and stories to become their form of understanding reality.

In this way the study of popular fictions not only reveals their symbiotic relationship with the ideology of the cultures they serve but also can enhance understanding of fictions which are commonly accepted as works of serious art. Such art asks us to look again at our familiar stories and to see—*through those stories*—reality as reality instead of reality shaped by narrative conventions. As noted in the first chapter, such art, to use the analysis of the process by the Russian formalist critic, Viktor Schlovsky, *defamiliarizes* the familiar (Jameson 43-98).

Walter Van Tilburg Clark's novel, *The Ox-Bow Incident,* places the reader squarely within an apparently conventional Western narrative. By doing so, he requires the reader to recall the idealistic and abstract message of the orthodox Western and to contrast that with the events— which represent *real* events and *real* life for a reader sympathetic with Clark—which take place in his fiction. A posse, impelled by mob mentality which cannot perceive true moral (or legal) guilt, trails three innocent men, accuses them of stealing cattle, and hangs them. The mob is led by a large rancher with money and power. The three accused 'rustlers' are pathetic and absolutely incapable of defending themselves, even though one, a man who has purchased a small herd of cattle, has the characteristics of an ideal colonist, i.e. a family, a need for a new beginning, a desire to better himself. In a 'normal' Western the hero would save the men at the last minute from the clutches of the rich and powerful villain, just as Gene Autry was able to save the farmers and ranchers oppressed by the wealthy and powerful businessman in "Rovin' Tumbleweeds" (1939) or as Roy Rogers was able to protect the sheepmen against the powerful cattlemen in "Roll on Texas Moon" (1946). Endowed with an unerring capacity to know truth and to impose justice, the hero would be able to reconcile the need for individual freedom (his own ability to act as an independent agent with moral vision superior to legal technicalities) and the need for service to civilized order (he would arrive in time not only to save the men from mob violence but also to guarantee them a proper trial).

No such figure arrives in the nick of time in *The Ox-Bow Incident.* Those able to understand events as they are taking place spend an uncomfortable amount of time meditating about justice and the human capacity to reason, but they are incapable of effective action. Those capable of action arrive too late. In an *Afterward,* written for the novel's paperback edition, Walter Van Tilburg Clark said that he tried in the novel to remind readers of the analogy between Nazi Germany's disregard for human rights, and the easy way procedures for justice were glossed over in the Western, wherein heroes have a moral sense that has something in common with the evil self-righteousness that led to the Holocaust.

In short, he self-consciously tried to force his readers to perceive the old, familiar story, the Western, in a new way, and to recognize that the ideology of the Western carried with it models for behavior which could be destructive.

The novel contradicts the comforting assumption of the Western that heroes have an intuitive vision of truth and justice *and* the capacity to act. The reality Clark reveals to the reader, compared with the idealistic and abstract message of the conventional Western recalled by the form of the novel, contrasts more sharply simply because it is realized by the reader in the form of a Western. The novel is not, strictly speaking, a parody, since parody connotes a humorous exaggeration of conventions and *The Ox-Bow Incident* has very little humor. It shares, however, elements with parody in that the expectations established by the pattern of events and the characters, the stolen cattle, the posse, the wealthy rancher, the weak colonists, the virtuous heroes, are violated in the extreme. Even the wealthy rancher isn't able to get his way entirely—although the weak and powerless are indeed hanged—but the heroes are also extremely incapacitated. In those extremes the novel shares with parody the drive to distort an original pattern that has become so familiar to its readers that they are unable to consider thoughtfully what the pattern communicates.

On a Public Broadcasting System television interview, E.L. Doctorow talked about the inception of *Welcome to Hard Times*. During the 1950s Doctorow was working as a script reader for a major Hollywood studio. His job required him to read numerous slick, conventionalized Western scripts. He saw that such stories had little to do with reality, that they in fact communicated a false way of seeing history. Partially motivated by anger with the rigid artificiality of the conventional narratives, he wrote *Welcome to Hard Times,* using elements from the many scripts he had read. Like Walter Van Tilburg Clark, he exaggerated elements from conventional Westerns in order to require readers to think about them in a new way. In a sense, like Clark, he parodies the conventional Western.

In a conventional Western, town building often constitutes a major part of the plot. In Louis L'Amour's *The Daybreakers* (1960), Orin and Tyrel Sackett overcome savagery, the wilderness, and the greed of an Easterner in order to build a town in New Mexico. Johannes Verne, the hero of *The Lonesome Gods* (1983), though emotionally drawn to life in the wilderness, dedicates himself to town building in the city of Los Angeles. Miss Nesselrode, of *The Lonesome Gods,* sees possibilities for growth and financial reward as Los Angeles, guided by energetic Yankees, develops as a population center. John Ford's film, "My Darling Clementine" (1946), "wholeheartedly celebrates the coming of law and order and civilization to the West in the form of [Henry] Fonda's [Wyatt]

Earp, the cowboy who gives up his nomadic existence and notions of personal vengeance to rid Tombstone of the anarchic Clantons" (Hardy 153). Westerns celebrate colonists grouping together to build churches and schools and thereby reaping the benefits of civilization.

Usually such towns in a Western are threatened by savagery, but happily men, such as the Sacketts or Wyatt Earp, trained in the ways of violence, save them. The narrator of Doctorow's novel, called the Mayor, a man who has failed to find a place for himself anywhere else, tries desperately to establish Hard Times, the name of the town in the novel. The Mayor earns his title simply because he assumes the role of record keeper for the shabby little community. The bulk of the novel consists of the efforts of the Mayor to create a family consisting of himself, Molly, and a boy whose father is killed by the villain in the initial episode. The Mayor's family never achieves love or understanding. The Mayor's efforts to make Hard Times into a town are equally futile.

Doctorow inverts the town building motif in *Welcome to Hard Times*. The novel begins with the destruction of the town by the Man from Bodie—a personified version of an overwhelming, uncivilized force that rapes and burns while the helpless townsfolk, including the Mayor, watch. Molly, who should have been the prostitute with the heart of gold in a standard Western, more or less like Kitty from the Gunsmoke television series, survives rape and terrible burns but becomes an embittered woman who can never forgive the Mayor for being a coward when she needed him. Throughout the fiction the exterior threat of the return of the Man from Bodie constitutes an omnipresent danger to the community, just as Molly's fierce, bitter nature constitutes an omnipresent danger to the 'family.' Only the Mayor seems foolishly optimistic enough to believe that the Man from Bodie won't return and that he and Molly will be able to help the boy to grow up to become a good man.

The West, in the Western narratives patterned on the way people in the United States *need* to see the West, provides for new beginnings; the Mayor has to believe that they can all begin again in the town of Hard Times. Molly has a less romantic view of the reality of the West. She is certain that the forces for civilization in the world are no match for the evil in the world. She knows the Man from Bodie will return. Eventually, when he does, the Mayor and some of the townspeople trap and wound him. Unfortunately, the Mayor, a civilized man, cannot club the Man from Bodie to death when he has the chance. Instead, he carries the villain to his dugout home. Molly, who should, according to the pattern of the Western, heal the bad man in spite of his evil deeds, tortures him savagely. Finally, the boy, the orphan the Mayor has tried to make into a good man, but who Molly has tried to make into a man violent enough to survive in the West, kills Molly as well as the Man from Bodie. At the end of the fiction the boy is out in the desert, having assumed the role of the Man from Bodie. The town is dead. Molly has the last word. Savagery triumphs over civilization. No hero arrives to impose order on the frontier. The effort to expand the United States frontier of settlement fails.

Such may or may not be a depiction of the truth of the real West of the nineteenth century. It is certainly not the familiar West of popular narrative which affirms that the forces of violence must eventually serve the needs of town building—even of such hard luck towns as Hard Times. By subverting the pattern for popular Westerns, Doctorow requires the reader to look at that familiar popular narrative and question the ideology it conveys. Indeed, given the international context which the expansionist frontier ideology of the Western nurtures, Doctorow's novel calls into question the optimistic concept of development, so popular as the policy of the United States toward Third World countries during the last several decades. Can nation building, i.e. development, be any more successful on the international level than town building in *Welcome to Hard Times?*

External Disorder on the Frontier: Little Big Man

The Ox-Bow Incident and *Welcome to Hard Times,* serious fictions indeed, seem technically rather simple. Both fictions create expectations based on the conventional Western and then violate those expectations to illustrate a philosophical position opposed to that communicated by the formulaic stories. Once the trick has been established one reads on knowing that conventional expectations will be denied for the sake of thematic statement. The two novels to be considered in the remainder of this chapter are both more sophisticated and far more subtle. For this reason they require more detailed attention.

In 1930 E. Douglas Branch wrote a widely accepted history of the frontier of the United States: *Westward: The Romance of the American Frontier.* Branch wrote a history, yet he labeled his study a *romance.* *Romance,* as the term is often used in the study of literature, characterizes fictions which have become highly conventionalized, so much so that they have only remote ties to the historical matter they pretend to depict. *Romance* is at the extreme narrative pole from history. *Romance* aspires to convey moral, ideological, or even supernatural truth. History aspires to convey factual, verifiable truth, the product of the rational examination of documents or testimony, even though the historian seeks to discover patterns in the facts from which he can abstract a more general, perhaps moral or ideological, kind of truth.

E. Douglas Branch found in the history of the frontier of the United States a pattern indicating the Anglo American's capacity to impose, before any form of recognized political power was official, a form of political order. Branch points out that as settlers moved into the Old Northwest (more commonly now considered the upper Middle West), they immediately began to survey the land, to divide it into townships, and to divide each township into 36 sections of land consisting of 640 acres (Branch 152-53). Anglo Americans, he insists, brought with them to the frontier the desire and the capacity to impose measure and a rational pattern upon the land, as well as the capacity to adapt in a rational way to a rational political organization. The Anglo American, in Branch's view, meant order. The Anglo American built houses, tilled the soil, established legal ownership, and made laws for conduct.

Branch provided visual images of that order by means of population density maps of non-indigenous populations which delineated the settled areas of the continental United States along the Eastern coast in dark shades or black, and the non-settled areas further West in lighter shades of gray and white. Various maps are interspersed through the book as the story is told of Anglo American colonists gradually installing their order over more and more territory.

Branch is quite open in his praise of the Anglo American's ability to bring order to the chaos of the West. He is innocently, it seems, covert about his assumption that such an order represents progress in the face of natural and human opposition over which a lesser people could not have triumphed. The Anglo American's march across the continent was, in Branch's mind, the inexorable march of progress signified by the imposition of law and order as conceived by the Anglo American. Perhaps, since *romance* suggests certitude, order, and clear distinction between modes of behavior considered right and wrong, it is appropriate that Branch should have chosen to label his history with the literary term *romance*.

Louis L'Amour, in interviews and written comments, insisted that his fictions were based upon factual, historically accurate detail. Still, like Branch, L'Amour wrote *romance*, for an ideological pattern governs his stories, and ideals are often not the stuff of reality. As we have seen, town building is a central motif in many L'Amour fictions. A L'Amour hero defeats the environment, Native Americans, and villains to establish a community patterned on European cultural systems. As such a hero enables the Anglo American population to expand, he enables orderly development. Town building requires populations; the town building motif in the Western is a sign, in a L'Amour novel, of the imposition of rational order upon the west.

Thomas Berger, author of *Little Big Man*, may or may not have ever seen Branch's history or read a novel by Louis L'Amour. However, there can be no doubt that Thomas Berger was aware of the extent and power of the perception of Anglo American domination as the imposition of rational order upon previous chaos, a view which could be found in numerous other history texts used in high schools and universities for many years. That concept is the target of Berger's satire. It is helpful to be aware of the extent and power of that view, the theme of histories such as E. Douglas Branch's *Westward: The Romance of the American Frontier*—as well as of the novels of Louis L'Amour—as one reads *Little Big Man,* if only to be more fully aware of the necessity for *Little Big Man* as one means for the liberation of readers trapped by mind-numbing clichés.

Berger's form of presentation satirizes the possibilities for historians, whether they call their works romance or novels. By extension, the form of presentation also satirizes any effort to impose rational order upon experience. Berger presents his story as the testimony of an observer, i.e. as oral history. However, the speaker (throughout most of the fiction) is a man who claims to be 111 years old, but whose doctors will only grant an age somewhere above 90. (One cannot help but think of L'Amour's many first person narrators who recall events one hundred years in the past while pausing, now and then, to comment upon contemporary—mid-twentieth century and later—trends or controversies.) Thomas Berger's ancient narrator is probably crazy. He lives in the psychiatric ward of a home for the aged. He is described as a paranoiac by his keepers.

The self-proclaimed 111 year old survivor of the Battle of the Little Big Horn, Jack Crabb, first comes to the attention of the 'editor' of his story, Ralph Fielding Snell, through observations made by Snell's practical nurse, a Mrs. Burr, who claims to have been Crabb's nurse when she worked at the home for the aged. Later the doctors at the home tell Snell that Mrs. Burr was merely a janitor, not a nurse at all. She is thus the first of three possible liars between the reader and the events that are narrated as history. The reader cannot be certain that any narrator's observations are truthful.

The second possible liar, Ralph Fielding Snell, scarcely reassures the reader as a reliable informant, although he professes to be a historian. He is a 52 year old hypochondriac who requires a nurse to bathe him after an operation on his nose. He is unmarried, dependent upon his 80 year old father for support, and he seems to have grave doubts about his sexual identity. Worst of all, for the reader of Westerns, he is an intellectual, given to pretentious language. In short, the story is introduced to the reader first by a coarse, uneducated woman, Mrs. Burr, who lies about her profession and snoops through her patient's personal belongings. She does not inspire trust. The story continues in the hands of a man with two last names, Fielding Snell—certainly a sign of pretense in the down to earth, straightforward world of the Western. This serpentine representation does not help to convince the reader of the authenticity of the events. We, as readers, believe, but even as we believe the story told us, primarily by Jack Crabb, we cannot help but feel that somewhere somebody is laughing at us for putting up with this

outrageously funny story being foisted upon us as oral history. The effect
makes us doubt the authenticity of history, indeed, of any effort to impose
meaning upon experience.

If there is little certitude to be found in the form in which the narrative
is presented, perhaps less may be found in the theme of the work. Usually
we extrapolate theme from the behavior of a hero or heroes. If we suspend
disbelief, if we accept a hero as a 'real' person, then we allow his or
her life to serve as an illustration for how life should be lived. We abstract
from the life of the hero a maxim, or description, which can be applied
to observable reality.

Jack Crabb is the central figure of the novel. A picaro and thus
a survivalist, Crabb is scarcely of the heroic mold in terms of the Western.
Two other characters are central. One, General George Custer, an
egomaniac, obsessed with his own perceptions of reality, refusing to admit
any evidence which might deter him from his suicidal battle at the Little
Big Horn, cannot be considered heroic—or a reliable informant. If there
is doubt about Crabb's sanity, there can be no doubt about Custer's
insanity. He will not see Native Americans when others see them (395).
When confronted with an obviously superior Native American force,
a village with an estimated warrior strength of 5,000 compared to his
own 300 troops, he asserts triumphantly that he has them at his mercy
since he has, he thinks, taken them by surprise (403). Jack Crabb, our
less than trustworthy narrator, tells us that Custer has lost his mind:
"Well, I expect Custer was crazy enough to believe he would win, being
the type of man who carries the whole world within his own head and
thus when his passion is aroused and floods his mind, reality is utterly
drowned" (404).

However, within his own peculiar world, Custer behaves consistently.
President Grant is his enemy, so at one point he threatens to kill Jack
Crabb whom he mistakes for Grant (in a slightly less than rational
moment even for a madman) (407). Yet he behaves with great valor,
even though, or perhaps because, he is mad. When his troops are pinned
down, facing death, he strides back and forth "calling me [Jack Crabb]
to fill a gap here, commending some others for holding on there, ever
confident and of good hope" (414-15). Crabb, who does not seem at
all mad at this time in his life, sees that Custer is exposing himself
to death in his gallant attempt to inspire the troops. Crabb pleads with
Custer to get down, but the General continues to behave inspirationally
if not very rationally. Crabb comments:

Well, his example might have been heartening to the ones who could see it. I recognized
he had gone crazy again, like when charging the ford alone, which surely accounted for
the failure of the arrows and lead to touch him, for missiles are reluctant to strike a
man who has gone out of himself by reason of madness or medicine (415).

Custer's madness takes a peculiar, culturally delineated form; he believes to the end in his own capacity to order life through reason. In the final moments of the battle (and of his life) he lectures, like a "genial scholar," in perfectly rational tones, as if he had the Native Americans locked in space, pinned to a slide for microscopic examination:

"Taking him as we find him, at peace or at war"—them arrows come swooshing down to stick upright all over dead men and horses—"at home or abroad," Custer goes amiably on, "waiving all prejudices, and laying aside all partiality, we will discover in the Indian a subject for thoughtful study and investigation" (418).

Custer's quirky rationalism requires him to think of the Native American as fixed in space, but all around him the arrows 'swoosh,' representing temporal flux. Caught up in defending himself, Crabb misses some of what Custer has to say, but as he is reloading his rifle he hears:

"It is to be regretted that the character of the Indian as described in Cooper's interesting novels is not the true one. Stripped of the beautiful romance with which we have been so long willing to envelop him, transferred from the inviting pages of the novelist to the localities where we are compelled to meet him, the Indian forfeits his claim to the appellation of the *noble* red man" (418).

Ever the sober scholar who believes the world can be examined and classified according to rule, Custer is, we are assured by crazy Jack Crabb, a hero, a man who "had worked out a style and...stuck to it" (429).

Crabb also tends to foist doubtful generalizations upon observation. A few days after the battle, Crabb and his now blind adopted Native American father, Old Lodge Skins, find the body of General Custer. Crabb says: "He was not scalped, Grandfather. The Indians respected him as a great chief."

Old Lodge Skins smiled...as at a foolish child.

"No, my son," says he. "I felt his head. They did not scalp him because he was getting bald" (435).

Old Lodge Skins, although certainly not normal to a reader acculturated by the same values which formed Custer's character, comes the closest of all of the characters to present both heroic behavior and a way of thinking about experience adapted to his world. He may (we cannot be certain) be a little crazy. Like Custer at Little Big Horn, Old Lodge Skins walks through a storm of gunfire at the Battle of Washita, evidently immune to the bullets of the enemy, just as Custer strode about, immune for a long time, to the arrows and bullets of the Native Americans. Yet as Old Lodge Skins nears death, he, like Custer when in similar straights, waxes philosophic from a cultural bias which seems to conform more closely to reality:

"...There is no permanent winning or losing when things move, as they should, in a circle. For is not life continuous? And though I shall die, shall I not also continue to live in everything that *is*?

"The Buffalo eats grass, I eat him and when I die, the earth eats me and sprouts more grass. Therefore nothing is ever lost, and each thing is everything forever, though all things move."

The old man put his knife into its beaded scabbard. He went on: "But white men, who live in straight lines and squares, do not believe as I do. With them it is rather everything or nothing: Washita or Greasy Grass. And because of their strange beliefs, they are very persistent" (441).

The old chief accepts life as an eternal, Bergsonian flux and thus is reluctant to elevate perception into patterns for thought. He is blind, but sees change (thinning hair) and time as the medium for life. Jack Crabb sees Custer's unscalped head and extrapolates a culture bound idea of the hero. Such a way of thinking, to Old Lodge Skins, leads to madness, and thus his last words: "Take care of my son here," he prays to the Great Everywhere, "and see that he does not go crazy" (445).

The capacity to avoid madness, according to *Little Big Man*, is the capacity to avoid dependence upon reason as the only means for apprehending the world. Certainly Custer, the extreme rationalist, is meant to be a cultural type. A parodic representation of the rational Anglo American, he cannot imagine a world beyond his own mental preconceptions. He perceives in fixed patterns, mad as a hatter.

Old Lodge Skins seems at some times to be but a parody of a pantheistic, fatalistic and superstitious Native American. Yet by accepting change and flux, he seems better adjusted to events than any of the other characters and/or narrators. Ralph Fielding Snell, the scholarly but effete historian who records Crabb's story, reveals himself incapable of dealing with everyday reality. The centenarian, Jack Crabb, whose veracity and mental health, questioned by all, seems not to have benefited in the least by Old Lodge Skins' prayer; he appears crazy, if for no other reason than for the fact that he chooses to admire poor crazy General Custer as a hero. He survives but, in spite of 111 years and his monumental story, he never really makes sense of his experience. If theme can be extrapolated from the narrative, it would seem to be that in an uncertain, changing world, the effort to impose man's reason on events signifies madness. Only Old Lodge Skins, who knows the nature of a world of change, understands that no patterns can ever be fixed upon experience.

Popular history, such as Branch's book, and popular fiction such as L'Amour's, while celebrating the benefits of rational Anglo American civilization for the West, glorify an ideology for domination. Old Lodge Skins' model for behavior on the frontier is a far cry from Branch's romance of the frontier, where sensible Anglo Americans survived because they were able to impose spatial order on the land, dividing it into townships and sections, living "in straight lines and squares" just as Old Lodge Skins lamented.

Branch's book, published in 1930, can scarcely be considered a best seller of the 1980s, certified by the market place as an expression of the frontier ideology of millions of readers. Yet, just behind his proclamation of the Anglo American's capacity to impose order on untamed space, and to maintain order therein, lurks the town building theme so familiar in the novels of Louis L'Amour, and behind that the familiar justification for the imposition of Anglo rule upon the West, Jefferson's agrarian vision—that from rational division of the land into small privately owned units, more appropriate and productive use of the land would ensue. The cowboy, the last frontiersman, led the way for the imposition of such order.

Associated with the Calvinist notion of the good steward in United States frontier ideology is the notion that man is somehow purified through contact with the soil. The United States began as a nation of farmers. Even today the concept of the family farm (although few know exactly what the phrase refers to) has sacred political implications: no politician from an agricultural state would dare to question the ideal of a man, a woman, and their children facing the elements in order to wrest a living from the land. The Anglo American's capacity to impose order upon the space of the West is a fundamental and sacred aspect of the ideology of the frontier of the United States.

Branch and L'Amour, in short, by idealizing the Anglo American's ability to impose political and spatial order on the frontier, appeal to concepts which are fundamental, and thus widely popular, in the United States. *Little Big Man* examines those assumptions, turns them on end in a very funny way, and forces readers to re-examine such ideas concerning the domination of Western space. The novel *defamiliarizes* the frontier for its readers. In *Little Big Man* Thomas Berger does the work of the literary artist.

Internal Disorder on the Frontier: Shane

In *Little Big Man* Thomas Berger directs his attention to the great open space of the West, to the space of the endless plains of the center of the nation, and how that space was confronted by two cultures in conflict. *Shane*, by Jack Schaefer, examines psychological space. *Shane* asks us to look closely at the frontier ideology of the United States and how patterns for manhood drawn from that ideology affect a boy's inner world—and perhaps the inner world of an entire culture as well.

Shane is often thought to be the prototypical Western. It does indeed incorporate conventional elements of the subgenre. Colonists, or homesteaders, led by Joe Starrett, confront the uncivilized, 'white savage' behavior of a rancher, Fletcher, who claims all of the land in a valley for himself. A frontier survivalist, Shane, rides into the valley, attempts to live a peaceful life helping the homesteaders with their work, but is finally driven to use his violent ways as a gunfighter to establish peace and justice. He then rides into the hills, presumably to repeat the same action in a new, still less civilized place. The setting is Wyoming—a state located in the West and, more importantly, in the *imagined* West of the United States. Wyoming is ranch country, the land of cowboys.

The characters are types familiar to fans of the popular Western; they would simply carry labels in the hands of a lesser writer. Joe Starrett is large and slightly clumsy, a typical 'sodbuster,' a type a reader of Westerns has met many times before. His spouse, Marian, a transplanted southern belle, dutiful, hard working, a loving wife and mother, is the pioneer woman, very familiar in the pages of a Western. The hero, Shane, could be no more than a cliché labeled *hero*. He has only one name, either first or last, the reader never knows. He has no defined past, no settled future plans, only a horse, a fancy gun, and a slightly faded aura of elegance. He expresses a desire to live in peace, but one knows from the beginning that he must use violence to protect the colonists. This might well be a set of characters and a situation for thousands of Western novels or films.

By insisting on the stereotypical nature of his story, Schaefer firmly identifies it as the same kind of story read and enjoyed by millions of Anglo Americans—a Western. He wants to take the reader inside the pattern. By doing so he can enable the reader to understand the importance of the narrative type as a key to the psychology of its audience. To establish the narrative as a Western was a simple task for readers well versed by mass media in the conventions of the fiction. To establish the importance of the story as a key to the psychology of its readers required a finer, more delicate, touch.

Shane is important as a key to understanding Anglo American culture because in the fiction the author demonstrates that as a cultural group Anglo Americans are doomed to psychological confusion about the nature of manhood and fatherhood. Anglo America has a civilized ideal of manhood embodied by the peaceful, work loving, gentle Joe Starrett, and it has an ideal of manhood embodied by the violent, or always potentially violent, Shane. We are, Schaefer tells us, a fatherless nation, doomed to be so because we can only know the blur of two fathers, in ways similar, but ultimately representing two distinct and conflicting ideal modes of behavior.

It is a profound observation and perhaps Schaefer could only fully demonstrate it by writing a Western. Within that familiar narrative pattern Schaefer had to establish the relationships between his characters with considerable care, for those relationships demonstrate the confusion concerning role models inherent in the Western. The story is told from the point of view of Joe and Marian's son, Bob, a young boy and therefore especially sensitive to models for emulation. For Bob, and thus for the reader, Shane and Joe Starrett, gunfighter and farmer, are presented as aspects of the same idea—father and hero. The two men form a metonymical extension of each other, each character standing for a part of the whole of father and hero. For Marion Starrett, Shane and Joe stand for a part of the whole of manhood and husbandhood. Both Shane and Joe love the boy, Bob, and each loves the wife, Marian. Each, in turn, is loved by the boy and by the woman. For the boy to say *father* is literally to denote Joe Starrett, but always with the suggested comparison with Shane. To recall Shane, on the other hand, is to suggest aspects of a potential, possible father. Shane and Joe Starrett share the role of father and hero for the boy, and since the boy tells us the story, the figure of the father as hero and the father as Shane blurs for the reader as well.

Action and events in the novel also blur the roles of Shane and Joe Starrett, violent hero and hard working farmer. Almost as soon as Shane enters the Starrett home he assumes a role normally associated with the head of the household. He takes Joe Starrett's place at the head of the table, a gesture which is explained later as necessary in order that he might remain always facing the entrance to the Starrett home. As a gunfighter and survivalist in the West he has learned that he must be on guard and watch the door to see who enters by keeping his back to the wall. Nevertheless this change, to which Joe Starrett acquiesces without argument, as if Shane did indeed belong at the head of the table, initially blurs the structure of the family. It would not be a significant incident if the boy did not give it significance. He does. By including the incident in the story, the boy narrator shares the confusion he feels about Shane and his father as hero and father.

Although Shane is very good at the farm work which he assumes when he agrees to become the Starrett's hired man, when Bob watches him he feels that such work is not right for Shane. Bob tells the reader, "you always felt in some indefinable fashion that he was a man apart...[that he] was shaped in some firm forging of past circumstances for other things" (34). At such times the boy senses the violence in Shane and is frightened. Occasionally Shane evinces a gunfighter's capacity for deadly concentration, but afterwards "he would be again the quiet, steady man who shared with father my boy's allegiance" (34).

Shane becomes a part of the family, which part the boy is not quite sure. "Though we had taken him in," he tells us, "you had the feeling that he had adopted us" (35). Prior to Shane's arrival the cowboys on the big Fletcher ranch had been Joe's romantic heroes, distant, seldom seen except when they galloped their horses down the road past the homestead. He had always held his father in a special, respected category.

After Shane's arrival he forgets about the cowboys and compares the two possibilities for manhood: "I wanted to be like him, [his father] just as he was...Now I was not sure. I wanted more and more to be like Shane..." (41).

The attitude of the other characters in the fiction also serves to unite the roles of the two men as leader and protector of the family. By hiring Shane, Joe Starrett made Shane a marked man, since Fletcher and his men see that they can destroy Joe Starrett by destroying Shane. Not only do their enemies, but also their friends see Shane and Joe Starrett as extensions of the same figure. When Fletcher's men taunt the other homesteaders, they begin to resent Shane since they think his presence has antagonized Fletcher.

> The effect showed, too, in the attitude our neighbors now had toward Shane. They were constrained when they called to see father and Shane was there. They resented that he was linked to them. And as a result their opinion of father was changing.(57)

Marian Starrett, it is soon made clear in the novel, is first smitten by Shane's southern charm and then falls deeply in love with him. The effect is to further merge the Shane/Joe Starrett figures as father and husband. The first morning Shane spends in the Starrett home his polite compliments on her cooking please Marian. As she urges Shane to stay with them until his horse has rested and the weather is better, seconding her husband's invitation, she "crinkled her nose at him the way she did when she would be teasing father,..." (11) and promises to bake a deep-dish apple pie. After talking with Shane about the latest fashions in population centers such as Dodge City and Cheyenne, she makes a hat in the style described by Shane and tries to attract the men's attention when they are working.

Later, when in a most understated way, she declares her love for Shane, which he acknowledges and reciprocates, the boy narrator allows the reader to further confuse the Shane/Joe Starrett patterns for manhood. Marian tells Shane that she has been wanting to talk to him when Joe was not around. "Yes, Marian," Shane replies, and the boy narrator interpolates: "He called her that the same as father did, familiar yet respectful, just as he always regarded her with a tenderness in his eyes he had for no one else" (64). The boy, the reader, and Marian Starrett are confused about the men's status in the family.

Through masterful and sensitive scenes in which the characters are developed, Schaefer blends Shane and Joe into the same figure. Together they open the fiction by working side by side to extricate a huge stump from the land, a symbol of a part of the land's untamed past which Joe could not master on his own. They fight side by side against Fletcher's tough cowboys in a classic (for the Western) saloon brawl. They are complete friends. Prior to the arrival of Joe at the saloon, Shane is badly beaten by a large number of Fletcher's men. After the fight, Joe carries Shane, "picked him up like he did me [the boy] when I stayed up too late and got all drowsy and had to be carried to bed" (77). Even the love his wife Marian feels for Shane does not disturb the unity of the men, not even when that love is acknowledged by the three of them. After the saloon fight, and after Marian has administered to the injuries suffered by the men, she makes the open secret explicit:

Her voice was climbing and she was looking back and forth and losing control of herself. "Did ever a woman have two such men?" And she turned from them and reached out blindly for a chair and sank into it and dropped her face into her hands and the tears came.

The two men stared at her and then at each other in that adult knowledge beyond my understanding. Shane rose and stepped over by mother. He put a hand gently on her head and I felt again his fingers in my hair and the affection flooding through me. He walked quietly out the door and into the night.

Father drew on his pipe. It was out and absently he lit it. He rose and went to the door and out on the porch. I could see him there dimly in the darkness, gazing across the river.

Gradually mother's sobs died down. She raised her head and wiped away the tears.

"Joe."

He turned and started in and waited then by the door. She stood up. She stretched her hands toward him and he was there and had her in his arms.

"Do you think I don't know, Marian?"

"But you don't. Not really. You can't. Because I don't know myself."

Father was staring over her head at the kitchen wall, not seeing anything there. "Don't fret yourself, Marian. I'm man enough to know a better when his trail meets mine. Whatever happens will be all right" (80).

Certainly, as he acknowledges that Shane can fulfill his part in the family as well, if not better, than he can, Joe Starrett contrasts with the standard male in the *macho* world of formulaic fiction. Later, facing the prospect of certain death, when he thinks he must go to town to confront Wilson, the hired gunman Fletcher has paid to kill him, Joe muses: "Things could be worse. It helps a man to know that if anything happens to him, his family will be in better hands than his own" (100). Joe's resignation to his fate, his acceptance of the fact that Shane is to assume his position as father and husband, certainly contributes to the reader's identification of both Shane and Joe with the social roles of father and husband.

As one may see, the love story in the novel is far more complex than that found in the standard Western. The story of the homesteader's triumph, by means of Shane's intervention with blazing six shooter, is scarcely in doubt; most readers know the story from its thousand time printed, filmed and televised versions, know it simply as the Western, not necessarily as *Shane* by Jack Schaefer, but as "Gunsmoke" or "Bonanza" or as a Clint Eastwood variation or a Louis L'Amour paperback. The resolution of the love relationships within the fiction is of far more interest and importance. To be sure, one can be fairly certain that even in a sophisticated Western, Marian will choose to be loyal and stay with Joe if he stays alive. After all, she is a good woman, and good women in a Western just don't run off with the hired hand.

What is at issue—and not resolved—is the question posed for the boy, and since the boy provides the reader with access to the story through his point of view, posed for the reader as well. What is it to be a man in the tradition of the frontier of the United States? Is the agrarian ideal, i.e. that a man is somehow purified by contact with the soil, by the struggle to dominate and make fruitful that which formally had been barren, a viable way to be? Such a pattern aggrandizes the stolid husbandry of Joe Starrett, with his peaceful concerns as a cattle breeder and farmer. Such a pattern celebrates the perfection of life within a given space. Or is the gunman, the man who knows that one must ever be alert to the potential savagery of others—and ever prepared to counter savagery with savagery—the one who one should call father and hero? Such a pattern celebrates domination of space as a means for survival, domination Shane can provide.

The duality leads to confusion, a confusion which the boy can only resolve in a strange Oedipal scene in which he assumes, for a time, the roles of both Shane and of Joe Starrett. The incident occurs after Shane has tricked Joe and knocked him unconscious in order to prevent him from facing Wilson, the hired gun, and certain death. Joe awakens after the boy, who has run the short distance to town and witnessed Shane's heroics, returns to the homestead. Joe Starrett learns that Shane has triumphed and, since he will henceforth be marked as a violent man in the valley, has ridden into the far hills—as the heroes in a Western are often required to do. Joe Starrett feels bereft, knowing that Shane will no longer be with them, and senses that their lives on the homestead will no longer be complete, even with the peace guaranteed them with the death of Fletcher and Wilson, both killed in the shoot-out. Starrett goes out into the night to stumble about and mull things over. Bob and his mother are alone. Marian lets Bob "crawl into her lap as [he]...had not done for three years or more" almost immediately after his return from witnessing Shane's heroism during the shoot out (114). She holds him after Joe has left the house until late in the night when, as the boy tells us:

...mother rose, still holding me, the big boy bulk of me, in her arms...She was holding me tightly to her and she carried me into my little room and helped me undress in the dim shadows of the moonlight through the window. She tucked me in and sat on the edge of the bed, and then, only then, she whispered to me: "Now Bob. Tell me everything. Just as you saw it happen" (116).

The boy does, thus vicariously becoming Shane for a time for his mother as he relives the time in the bar, and then he falls asleep. The next morning he awakens to find the bed still warm where his mother had slept. Both of the father figures are absent; in their absence the boy seems to assume their roles as his mother's lover.

Assigning the events at the end of the novel such a diagrammatic Oedipal configuration may seem to some to be inferring far more that Schaefer intended. One cannot know exactly what Schaefer intended. The ways of the imagination are not always clear while we are creating or even in retrospect. Yet the divided father and husband figure has been given considerable and considered attention throughout the novel. With one father (Shane) gone into the far hills, and the other father (Starrett) wandering weakly about the farm, the time is right for the boy to be complete, for a while being both Shane and Joe with his mother. The fact remains, of course, that the boy cannot sustain that role. The incident underscores the effect of the divided father, the undefined role of the male, which Schaefer has stressed throughout his examination of the psychological implications of the frontier story of the United States.

What is it to be a true man in the United States? Schaefer does not answer the question posed by the ménage on the Starrett farm, a ménage perhaps symbolic of a psychological confusion in the United States that reaches far beyond the homestead represented in the novel. By insisting on the conventions of the Western, Schaefer demonstrates the timeless nature of the action. The syntax of the Western plot is synchronic, outside time. What takes place in *Shane* insofar as action is concerned has taken place thousands of times in the imaginations of those who read Westerns in the United States, and that is a very large proportion of the population. By examining with such delicacy the psychology of the characters in the novel, Schaefer suggests one very important way in which the fiction may reflect a profound psychological problem for many who depend upon the pattern of the Western fiction as means for processing information about the world. Since that fiction is the Western, normally associated with assured, dynamic action based on the hero's survival skills, Schaefer's story shows us something entirely new about the subgenre, and about what the Western means for its readers.

There was an excellent film made from the novel, a film surprisingly close to the novel. Although few commentators seem to have thought the love relationships to be as important as presented herein, the film takes careful note of the complexity of the love story. At the film's end the boy calls after Shane who is riding into the moonlight. He calls Shane's name over and over, begging him to come back. Of course, true to the conventions to the very end, Shane does not return. But for a time the boy, and the audience which identifies with the boy, stand calling after Shane, our violent father, to come back to assure us peace in which we can profess our love for our other father, the man of peace. Far too often, our history tells us, Shane, or what he represents, *has* returned. Perhaps he is never too far away.

Schaefer uses the fictional pattern about the frontier in order to require his readers to reflect upon the serious sociological and psychological problems for a nation that has some of its most fundamental beliefs reaffirmed by reading and viewing Westerns.

The ideology of the Western demands that the hero have infallible moral vision and the violent means to enforce that vision. Walter Van Tilburg Clark shows how close the Western, insofar as the question of justice is concerned, is to Nazism. The Western, according to E.L. Doctorow, maintains a false sense of optimism concerning the basic goodness of man and his ability to wash away the past and begin again in a new place. Conventional frontier ideology, such as that found in E. Douglas Branch's history and Louis L'Amour's novels, extols the Anglo American's ability to impose patterns upon space while Thomas Berger shows us that such rational patterns force us into a form of madness. Jack Schaefer shows us the psychological confusion he finds inherent in the myth of the West.

Walter Van Tilburg Clark, E.L. Doctorow, Thomas Berger, Jack Schaefer—all wrote very serious novels. They certainly all share a very serious, and pessimistic, view of frontier ideology in the Western. Is that pessimistic vision any more true for having been presented in sophisticated fictions, technically far superior to the average Western novel, fictions which can engage the attention of Professors of English who can find all kinds of 'hidden' meanings therein? Do these men—the novelists, not the professors—know more and see more deeply than Louis L'Amour or Zane Grey or the men who wrote the scenarios for Gene Autry? Does esthetic accomplishment demonstrate a firmer grasp of truth? The answer is Yes. Not *yes* because the 'serious' authors know more about the final reality of what happened in the West during the nineteenth century, but rather *yes* because they see that to grasp truth, of any sort, however tentative, one must first escape the grasp of fictions—of lies. To the extent that the Western has become a conventionalized, abstract way of realizing history it has become a form of a lie. In order for readers to escape that lie they must be shown how those patterns dominate the way they understand their past and themselves. The works surveyed in this chapter help readers to break the grasp of fictions. In that way they put readers closer to the truth than the frontier ideology sustained by popular Westerns.

Chapter VII
Caudillaje Defamiliarized:
Sarmiento, Vargas Llosa, Asturias, and Yáñez

National Disorder: Facundo *and* Caudillaje

Serious Latin American writers, like serious Anglo American writers, invite their readers to examine accepted views of reality embodied in the fictions of their culture. Such fictions form patterns for the way people relate to one another and govern themselves. The literary artists discussed in this chapter ask readers to examine the ways of *caudillaje*, an aspect of Latin American culture which popular prose and image literature help to sustain.

As we have seen, conventional fictions in Latin America require the hero to use violent means to enforce order upon a disordered frontier, to personify a strength that represents a divine, omnipotent power existing outside time. Estefanía's heroes, operating as representatives of a central, powerful individual, carry with them, in the strength of their whips, fists, and guns, the capacity to impose order. Such order is *personal* order, an order sustained by the strength of one person. Such order may be imposed through extensions of the *caudillo's* personal power, by means of relatives or close and loyal followers. But once that person grows too weak or dies, his personal order no longer exists. Sooner or later, in a culture in which *caudillaje* prevails, a new personal order must be imposed.

For this reason Estefanía's fictions do not progress in time. His heroes resolve a problem, impose order, and then move on. However, once they have moved on, the potential for disorder exists. The order that was imposed was the result of their personal abilities to implement their power, with guns, with whips, with guile, or with sheer strength of personality—the capacity to make others respect and even fear them simply by the force of their presence. In the same way, Aquila Solitaria, in the strength of his own person, gives order to a chaotic frontier world. In frequent episodes he resolves problems in a village, thus suggesting that he has given peace to an entire area. However, since the hero embodies the only source for order, his absence allows the forces of disorder and bad behavior to assert themselves once again. As in the works of Estefanía, events in *Aquila Solitaria* do not progress in time. He, and his enemies and the people he helps, live outside time.

Facundo: Civilización y Barbarie, Domingo Sarmiento's 1845 historical novel, provides an important point of departure for an examination of *caudillaje* in serious literature. In his novel Sarmiento dissects the characters and behavior of two notorious Argentine *caudillos,* Juan Facundo Quiroga and Juan Manuel Rosas. Facundo Quiroga rose from a ranch hand, a gaucho, to become the most powerful man in Argentina. After Facundo Quiroga's assassination, following a period of extreme disorder, Juan Manuel Rosas was asked to rule the country. He demanded and was given absolute power.

Sarmiento's historical biography of the two *caudillos* deals directly and chronologically with the characteristics of the men and the conditions that brought them to power. In the process it explores the characteristics of *caudillaje* and the conditions which foster such a form of government. As has been noted, Facundo Quiroga began as a gaucho on the Argentine pampas. Juan Manuel Rosas, according to Sarmiento, came from the mountain hinterlands. Sarmiento establishes, over and over again, that both Facundo Quiroga and Rosas belonged to the country, to the pampas and the mountains, and that both distrusted the qualities of civilization to be found in men of the cities.

To maintain power, Sarmiento tells us, the *caudillo* creates a sense of fear among those about him. Since he is incapable of proper government—of self or of country—he uses terror as an expedient. His sudden, impetuous actions inspire respect. Using his natural wiliness, a capacity for observation and the credulity of the people, he makes those around him think that he has divine powers, that he is able to see further into events—even to actually foretell events. By these means he creates a supernatural aura about himself in order to gain and keep the respect of the people and his power over them (66-71).

The system of *caudillaje* allows the *caudillo* to possess his country—not only the property but the people as well. Sarmiento notes that, after Facundo was killed, "Rosas was not content this time to demand dictatorship, the extraordinary faculties, etc. No, that which he asked for is what the phrase [the sum of public power] expresses: traditions, customs, forms, guaranties, laws, culture, ideas, consciousness, life, ranches, preoccupations;...all that which has power over society and that which resulted would be the sum of public power he demanded" (182). With the *sum of public power,* Juan Manuel Rosas became, in effect, the owner of the people and the property in the country.

Thereafter Rosas managed people just as he managed his cattle on his cattle ranch. The fiestas of each parish were like roundups. The red sashes, which all were required to wear as evidence of their patriotism (or, in other words, their loyalty to Rosas), were like brands on the cattle.

People learned to obey, to be enthusiastic when they should be enthusiastic, to applaud when they should applaud, to be quiet when they should be quiet. Representative government became null, for, "With the possession of the *sum of Public Power,* the House of Representatives becomes useless, for in fact laws emanated directly from the *person* of the chief of the Republic" (192).

As we have seen in the popular novels and comics books, and in cultural history, people want the *caudillo* to provide governmental order. As Sarmiento *defamiliarizes* popular concepts of the *caudillo,* as he imposes his *words* upon the simplifications of the popular image in the public mind, he demonstrates how Facundo Quiroga and Rosas brought disorder instead of order. When Facundo, the barbaric genius, took power, "the traditions of the government disappeared, the forms were degraded, the laws became a game in heavy hands, and in the midst of this destruction effected by the hooves of the horses, nothing was substituted, nothing was established...Facundo desired to possess, yet was incapable of creating a system of taxation, to arrive at that which all governments, heavy or imbecilic, always arrive" (76). After Facundo took over Cuyo and La Rioja, "Never had the two cities suffered equal catastrophes, not only for the evils done directly by [Facundo] Quiroga, but for the disorder of all business which led to the emigration in mass of [civilized] people" (138). With Facundo in power, people lived in terror. Gangs roamed and beat citizens. People were afraid to go out (171).

The personality of the *caudillo* dominates all in a system of *caudillaje.* His world must be a reflection of himself. Sarmiento tells us: "Egoism is behind nearly all great historical characters; egoism is the port from which are executed all great actions. [Facundo] Quiroga possessed this political gift in an eminent grade, and exercised it in concentrating in his possession all that which he saw disseminated in the uncultivated society which surrounded him: fortune, power, authority, all that was with him; all that which he could not acquire, manners, instruction, real respectability, he persecuted [and] destroyed in the persons who had them" (78-79).

The *caudillo* completely dominates. According to Sarmiento, from 1835 to 1840 almost the entire city of Buenos Aires passed through the jails, many remaining prisoners for up to six months. This was Facundo's way of disciplining the city and its people. By the time Rosas took over, the city was accustomed to such domination. In 1844 Rosas was able to "present to the world a people which had but one thought, one opinion, one voice, an enthusiasm without limit for the person and the will of Rosas" (79-80)!

The incidental quirks of the *caudillo* become means by which the people are governed. For example, Facundo loved to gamble. After he achieved power he invited (demanded) that people play with him. It was a system of expoliation. "No one received money in La Rioja, no one possessed it, without being invited immediately to play and to leave it in the power of the *caudillo*" (81).

Facundo possessed La Rioja as an absolute and arbitrary owner. "There were no other voices than his, no other interests than his. Since there were no writers, there were no opinions, and since there were no diverse opinions, La Rioja was a war machine which went where he took it" (83).

According to Sarmiento, the system of *caudillaje* requires *caudillos* to be savage. Both Facundo and Rosas became renowned for their brutality. On one occasion Rosas made a leather strap into shackles which he put on foreign agents in order to teach them a lesson. Rosas had learned from another mountain man *caudillo* how to *enchalecabar* his enemies; that is, to tie them within a fresh hide and leave them abandoned while the hides slowly stiffened and contracted, eventually killing the victim. Often Rosas chose to execute men by cutting their heads off with knives rather than simply to shoot them (47).

By managing information, which, in many cases simply meant keeping most of the people uninformed and isolated, Rosas managed public opinion and maintained his power. He dismantled the postal system in Argentina (198). He knew that ignorant and uninformed people were easier to govern. Beneath a *caudillo's* strong hand, without access to information and contact with people from other parts of the world, people live outside time, in a world wherein tradition becomes ever more entrenched, and as it deepens its hold on the people, so it sustains the power of the *caudillo*.

Rosas also knew how to manage international media. He managed to convince foreign reporters that his strong hand was in the best interest of international investment, so that it "was repeated, on the order of Rosas, in all of the European press, that he was the only one capable of governing in the semi-barbaric countries of America" (215).

Rosas knew how to use, and abuse, language as a means to control people. Prior to his assumption of power, the *Unitario* political party had urged centralism, which many associated with the system of power which preceded independence from Spain. Nevertheless, the *sum of public power*, with which Rosas had been invested by Buenos Aires, was extended to all of the Republic. In effect, the nation became *unitarian* beneath the power of Rosas. However, it was *not* said that it was the unitarian system which Rosas had established, of which the person of Rosas was the center, but rather that a federation of states, each with powers of its own, formed the government. Thus people rallied to the cries of *long live the federation* and *death to the unitarios.* The word *unitario* stopped being the distinctive name of a political party and began to express all that which was hated (196).

Temporal and Spiritual Disorder: La Casa Verde

Molded by traditional and popular culture, many in Latin America still believe that *caudillos* and *caciques* bring order to disordered hinterlands. Contemporary serious fictions, such as Vargas Llosa's *La Casa Verde,* like Sarmiento's *Facundo,* attempt to demystify the *caudillo* by depicting him as a force for disorder and chaos. It is that disorder, temporal and spiritual, which Vargas Llosa focuses upon in *La Casa Verde.* An analysis of the plot of *La Casa Verde* clearly illustrates that the *caudillo,* Don Julio Reátegui, and his desire for profit, are the source of the people's misery, confusion, and degradation.

The novel is set on a twentieth century Peruvian frontier, at a meeting place between two cultures often in conflict with each other. Santa Maria de Nieva, a village located at the junction of two rivers, the Nieva and the upper Marañón, is the primary point of contact in the novel between Native Americans and non-indigenous people. Down river are violent waterfalls and two military posts. The town confronts Native Americans and the jungle, the "furious onslaught of the vegetation" (20). On the edge of town, close to where a river pilot, Adrián Nieves, a central figure in the novel, lives, people dump their trash. Once a week the Mayor's workers burn it. During the week people from the Aguaruna tribe "come to eat in the place..., and some of them dig into the garbage looking for...items that can be used at home..." (37).

The novel opens with a frontier encounter. The incident illustrates the moral confusion on the frontier where two Peruvian cultures—the indigenous and the European—confront each other. Escorted by a scruffy bunch of soldiers, Fats (who only thinks of sex), Blondy, Blacky and the Sergeant, Sister Angélica and Sister Patrocinio, driven by their mission to evangelize, go up river to search for Aguarunas in order to kidnap children to save their souls (3). On the river Adrián Nieves guides them. On shore they find a "handful of huts with conical roofs, small plots of cassava and bananas, and thick undergrowth all around. Among the huts, small trees with oval-shaped pockets [hung] from the branches..." (4). The people appear and the nuns talk to them. Meanwhile the soldiers are sexually aroused by the young Native American girls (5). When the nuns give the Aguaruna people food and trinkets—mirrors and necklaces and colored beads—the soldiers believe the whole effort foolish and a waste of time, for they see the Aguarunas as no better than animals.

Eventually, the nuns give orders as the Natives prepare to leave. Shorty and Blondy are charged to take care of the little girls, with orders not to commit any 'brutalities' (12). One of the soldiers fights with the old woman who has been guarding the two girls, but Blondy drags the girls away.

The actual kidnapping is done with the "Hail Mary" being intoned by a totally disembodied narrator, while guns are held on the Aguaruna men. Two soldiers fight with an old woman as one soldier drags the girls away (13). The words of the prayer recall the misguided spiritual efforts of the nuns and, given the context, holds their religious endeavors to the sharp light of satire as the girls and the soldiers struggle, emphasizing the violent nature of the confrontation. The sound of the prayer behind the visual struggle creates sensory confusion, perhaps equivalent to the various levels of moral confusion the characters and, indeed, the reader, experience throughout the scene. The nuns are acting in good faith, even if foolish good faith. The soldiers are little better than animals; the Aguarunas are helpless. When one of the nuns, Sister Angélica, goes to help one of the soldiers struggling with one of the girls, another girl hits the nun and the soldier, Blondy, asks, "what did he tell her,...Sister, wasn't she an animal" (14)? The de las Casas and Sepúlveda controversy concerning the Native Americans as beasts or human beings with potentially Christian souls has been clearly defined but in twentieth-century form, one which would appear to have been influenced by the plastic techniques of presentation of sound and scene available on the screen.

The incident opens the novel but it does not initiate the action of the novel. The reader must eventually discern that certain incidents narrated later have preceded the opening incident in the novel. Isolated from the time of the world, sequential time does not exist for people in hinterlands dominated by a *caudillo*. Set apart by geography as well as politics, they live lives whose confusion can be suggested by a non-sequential narrative form. The reader thereby achieves a sense of the timeless and formless life of a frontier world dominated by the power of one man.

However clear the initial frontier conflict, the narrator does *not* allow the reader to form clear cause and effect relationships between events and characters as he depicts the confusion of his frontier world. Highly indirect narrative exposition reveals that Don Julio Reátegui controls the rubber trade in the upper Peruvian Amazon during World War II. Yet Don Julio Reátegui, certainly a main character in the novel, *appears* to act almost peripherally. He is not the official governor of the province, yet he controls the governor and imposes his power wherever it is necessary in order to maintain profitable trade with the Native Americans. The rubber sold through his channels goes at his price for enormous personal profit.

As in popular comics, such as *Aquila Solitaria,* foreign influence poses a threat to the community. It also poses a threat to the control of the *caudillo.* Influenced by the counsel of two itinerant Spanish teachers, the Native Americans threaten to form a cooperative to sell directly to foreign buyers. At this point Don Julio must take a firm stand to protect his interests.

The reader apprehends much of the novel through the point of view of Fushia, a Japanese immigrant who at one time received contraband rubber for Don Julio Reátegui. Reátegui, the *caudillo,* against governmental policy which supported the United States in the war against Japan, sold rubber to the Japanese, using Fushia as his intermediary. In order to get money to run away after having been caught, Fushia gets Lalita, his fiancé and later his wife, to whore with Reátegui. Nevertheless, Lalita follows Fushia (79-83). A faithless husband, Fushia fornicates with Native American women in the camp where he and Lalita live. He is also physically cruel to his wife. He tells his story in flashback as Aquilino, a canny old river man who has befriended him for reasons unimaginable to this reader, takes the former rubber buyer—by that time terribly ill from leprosy—down river to a leper colony. His leprosy seems almost a just reward, or at least a physical sign of his moral decay. However, Fushia's morality is but an extension of the *caudillo's* morality, his cruelty an extension of the cruelty of the *caudillo.*

The narrative method used to tell Fushia's story mirrors the moral confusion of his life. Fushia's mind wanders as he journeys with Aquilino down river and as his mind wanders, so does the narrative. In mid-paragraph, on the river on their way to the leper colony, as Fushia responds to a remark from Aquilino, the scene shifts to Dr. Portillo and Don Fabio Cuesta and Don Julio Reátegui. Fushia has recalled a scene when he was working for Don Julio and complains about the way a man named Portillo and Don Julio had abused him socially in Iquitos, the city where Don Julio had his main office. The scene then shifts completely from the river to past events as the point of view becomes totally that of Fushia's recollections. Don Julio is the boss of the region. He has made Don Fabio governor and together they have paid off enough people to gain control of the rubber business. But bandits are operating in the region and they aren't getting all of the rubber.

The presentation almost defies the realization of any causal relationship between events, but in reconstruction it is clear that the *caudillo,* Julio Reátegui, has been at the center of the moral decay in the narrative (115-120). Fushia's reminiscence of the time of the rubber bandits concerns a time after Fushia had run away but before he had became ill with leprosy. Fushia, with the help of the Huambisa tribe, has been stealing rubber from the Aguarunas, who usually trade with Don Julio Reátegui, and so he has been stealing the money and trade of his former employer. He and Aquilino, along with a drug addict, Pantancha, are the rubber bandits. The disordered past and present relationships of the characters underscores the existent disorder between races and cultures on the frontier.

What order the *caudillo* imposes on the Peruvian frontier between the Native Americans and the European people derives from brutality. Not only has Don Julio been losing trade due to theft, but the Aguarunas have been withholding rubber for sale through cooperatives. Don Julio, with Corporal Roberto Delgado and other soldiers, goes to talk to the Aguarunas. Having encountered them, after a bit of ceremony, Don Julio goes forward, ostensibly in peace to greet their leader, a man named Jum. When the two men are close, Don Julio slowly takes his flashlight, lifts it, as if it were a gift, and then hits Jum with it. The soldiers then attack and capture the Native Americans.

A small girl clings to Jum's legs at this time. The little girl becomes Bonifacia, raised by the nuns, later to be the wife of the Sergeant (Lituma) and, still later, a whore in the Green House in Piura. Her life is ultimately destroyed by this intrusion into the Native American world by Don Julio (122-124).

The *caudillo*, Don Julio Reátegui, must possess all within his control, and the drive to possess crushes those who do not submit to his power. Jum, the Aquaruna struck down by Don Julio's blow with the flashlight, has his life destroyed by the *caudillo's* intrusion. Having been captured, he tries to defend himself from trumped up charges. Don Julio attacks him because he wants to know why Jum has not sold rubber to Don Julio's employee. Jum tells him his people have formed a cooperative and plan to sell directly in Iquitos. Don Julio orders Jum to sell to Boss Escabino (Don Julio's buyer) and not to a cooperative. Jum calls Don Julio the Devil (145-148).

Meanwhile, the soldiers catch Bonifacia and take her to the Governor. She is not injured, but given to the nuns in Santa Maria de Nieves to be educated and made into a Christian. Later, after she has grown up a bit, Don Julio tries to obtain her to be a servant in his home.

Like the *caudillo* Rosas from Sarmiento's *Facundo,* Don Julio Reátegui believes it best to keep those under his rule ignorant of outside events and, essentially, removed from the temporal flow of the rest of the world. There are a variety of times and places present in the narrative on the same pages, giving the reader a sense of an overlaying of events and time, as if all time were present and all events simultaneous, as if the people in the hinterlands living beneath the rule of the *caudillo* know no sequential time in which some form of progress might take place.

Much later, for example, in terms of the sequence of events in the narrative, although not in terms of the sequence of presentation, Jum complains to the Army authority, a new Lieutenant, in Santa Maria de Nieva, telling him what had happened to give Don Julio Reátegui a guise for his accusations. Jum can barely make himself understood since he does not speak Spanish very well. Jum seems out of his proper time and place, an anachronism. The present time of the narration is when the new Lieutenant is listening to the Sergeant. The past time of the narration is when Don Julio brought Jum in and Jum tried to explain himself.

All this precedes a flash forward in the same paragraph to the Lieutenant tying his shoes as the Sergeant briefs him. Jum, the Sergeant says, doesn't do anything bad—just keeps complaining and won't leave the town. He, the Native American, is indeed an anachronism. He has complained to the former Lieutenant to no avail and now, with the new Lieutenant, wants to try again, to protest the occasion, now long past, when his tribe was captured and the men beaten and he had been brought in for punishment, when he had been tied between two trees in the middle of the town and beaten by Don Julio and his soldiers. Mid-paragraph again, Jum complains about being thirsty and Corporal Delgado—who was immediately in charge at the time Jum was taken—tells him he cannot have water, that whoever should give him food or water will answer to him.

Then the reader is taken forward in time, to the time of the new Lieutenant, and Adrián Nieves steps forward to interpret for the now freed, but broken, Jum, who can never escape the trauma, and thus the time, of his capture and torture at the hands of Don Julio Reátegui. Adrián Nieves talks to Jum and tells the Lieutenant that Jum cannot go back to his village until they give him back everything they took from him. Jum tries to tell them of the way they were treated when Don Julio came to their village and of the way Bonifacia was taken by Don Julio. The Lieutenant cannot understand.

There are, at this point, three *times* present in the narrative—the time of the attack by Don Julio and the soldiers on Jum's village, the time of Jum's punishment in Santa Maria de Nieva, and the most recent time, the time of the arrival of the new Lieutenant, who tries to understand Jum's complaint. Jum, in the present, with the new Lieutenant, being interpreted by Adrián Nieves, doesn't want to go back to his village without the "rubber, the hides, the primers, [a set of books given his tribe by the Spanish teachers] and the girl, Bonifacia, so they [his tribesmen] would see that Jum was right" (182).

It is worth noting that Jum, at the time of being hanged between the two trees, called for the two teachers who, Corporal Delgado says, were subversive agitators, which, the Corporal says, was why Jum had attacked Corporal Delgado on his previous visit to the village prior to the expedition with Julio Reátegui when Jum had been taken. Outsiders, those who interfere within a region or a country, cause confusion for the *caudillo* and for indigenous people.

Jum, apparently naive, believes the government in Lima is a source for justice and that the new Lieutenant, a representative of the government, can give him justice. Ultimately, the Lieutenant announces that Don Julio and the Corporal had gone too far, but that the Army could do nothing now. He tries to trick Jum by giving him a piece of newspaper that supposedly tells him that if he finds Don Julio and Escabino (the now dead former rubber buyer for Don Julio) they will make everything right. Of course Jum sees that the Lieutenant simply wants to put him off. He therefore tears the paper up as soon as he leaves the Lieutenant's office.

At this point the narrative shifts again to the time when Jum was being punished between the trees, immediately after having been taken prisoner by Don Julio Reátegui. The punishment over, he is told to leave, but obviously nothing can be over for Jum. His life having been destroyed when he was arrested and taken from his people, he now lives outside time, outside change, for he can never recover the continuity of his life, the continuity from which he was wrenched by the *caudillo*, Don Julio Reátegui.

The passage illustrates the temporal and psychical damage the *caudillo* inflicts upon the people of the frontier. Isolated from contact from outsiders, who can make hinterland people less dependent and subject to the control of the *caudillo*, and isolated from progress by being denied education, they live as anachronisms, outside time, and, as civilization encroaches, increasingly without place (172-187). Don Julio Reátegui is a far cry from the benevolent *caudillos* of the imagination of the readers of M.L. Estefanía who, through the violent acts of their representatives, always set things right.

Since the *caudillo* possesses all power, individuals are unable to achieve more than transient control over their own lives. For a limited time on the frontier people are able to achieve dignity and honor, but it is a fragile state, always in danger. Bonifacia, having grown up in the Mission with nuns, has a position of responsibility over the new little girls brought in from the villages. Overcome by pity for two little Native American girls taken from their families to be Christianized, she has helped them escape and, as punishment, has been expelled from the mission. She has found a home with Adrián and Lalita. Sergeant Lituma, Adrian's friend, meets Bonifacia and soon proposes to her in order to assure his, and her, honor.

Thus, beyond the direct and immediate impact of the *caudillo*, people live on the frontier with honor and dignity. It is the power of the *caudillo* that forces them into confusion and misery. The story of Bonifacia and Adrián and Lalita, presented directly, in an almost reportial style, conveys a sense of the dignity and grace available to those who, at least for the time, are outside the reach of the law dominated by the *caudillo*.

Aquilino's relationship with others speaks for the dignity available to the frontiersman in Peru. Before becoming an outlaw rubber trader with Fushia, shortly after Bonifacia moves in with Adrián and Lalita, Aquilino arrives at the dock in Santa Maria de Nieva with his raft, a floating store from which he sells household items and material. Bonifacia, who is the fiancé of the Sergeant, sees the old man, Aquilino, watches the women buy, and then in the evening goes aboard and begs him to give her some yellow cloth for her wedding dress. Having just been expelled from the mission, she has no work and no money, only the charity of Adrián and Lalita. Aquilino goes to visit his friends, Adrián and Lalita. He is a kind man. He plays with the children, gives gifts, then gives Bonifacia the yellow cloth.

Nevertheless, the dominance of the *caudillo*, Don Julio Reátegui, eventually causes the characters in the fiction to fall from whatever momentary grace they achieve living near their jungle home. Eventually, all of them become regulars at Chunga's Green House, a tawdry night club and whore house in Piura, a small city down river from the frontier village, Santa Maria de Nieves. Chunga's Green House, like those who frequent it, has an innocent and honorable past. Anselmo, who later we learn comes from the jungle, arrives in Piura a stranger but has money and makes many friends. After a time he goes to the edge of the desert, just past the area of town reserved for Blacks, and builds a large green house, in which, in due time, he establishes a number of prostitutes. The establishment is well managed and respectable. Anselmo continues to have the important men of the city as friends, with the exception of Father García, the local priest, who sees him as an incarnation of Satan.

Anselmo is totally independent, without past, without commitments to anyone. Perhaps because he comes from the jungle, he is free from the sexual constrictions of the Western world, embodied by Father García. Anselmo is free to love where love takes him, without regard for conventions. After an indeterminate number of prosperous years as proprietor of the Green House—painted green, Bonifacia suggests, in honor of Anselmo's past life in the jungle—Anselmo falls in love with Toñita, a mute, blind orphan child much loved by the people in the city. He takes her to live with him in the Green House in his own special apartments. She is never part of the business of the whore house.

Anselmo, even then, has the aura of a saint. He is an accomplished harpist and plays for his patrons.

Father García discovers that the aging Anselmo has taken to his bed the young, blind orphan girl from the town, Toñita, the girl who many believe to be especially blessed, and has fathered a child with her, which, tragically, leads to the girl's death while giving birth. In a rage against what he sees as the personification of Satan in his town, Father García burns the Green House to the ground. Anselmo, broken hearted from the loss, not of his whore house but of his beloved Toñita, falls from his position of grace and dignity in the town. He sleeps on the street and begs his living. Years later he recovers somewhat and is able to play his harp in the new green house, a much less ostentatious whore house run by his daughter, a lesbian called Chunga, the child born of Toñita at her death. Chunga's Green House is just a honky tonk on the fringe of the city.

It is to this new, sordid Green House that the characters who lived decent lives in Santa Maria de Nieves or in the jungle eventually descend. The events, which began when Don Julio intruded into the lives of the Native Americans, end in Chunga's miserable Green House.

The moral degradation of the characters emphasizes a sense of a temporal and spatial break in the action. The central characters change. It is almost as if one is reading about entirely different people in entirely different worlds. However, little by little one comes to know that Chunga's Green House is but a debased version of Anselmo's grand Green House, just as the characters at Chunga's are but debased, and older, versions of the same characters first met in Santa Maria de Nieves.

The *caudillo's* intrusion has not only failed to give order to the frontier but has fathered great social disorder. At Chunga's, the Sergeant, transferred from Santa Maria de Nieves back to his home town, Piura, is known as Lituma. He gets into a silly game of Russian roulette with a rancher and the rancher is killed. For what is assumed to have been a crime, the Sergeant is sent to prison. While he is gone, Bonifacia is unable to earn her living. Josefino, supposedly a friend of Lituma (the Sergeant), insists on taking Bonifacia to his place. When they get there other friends of Lituma (the Sergeant) are there, drunk, in the dregs of an all night party in its worst stage (348-354).

Afterwards Josefino begins to pimp for Bonifacia, who becomes a whore and works at Chunga's Green House. There she becomes known as Wildflower, a reference to her former life in the jungle. When the Sergeant returns from prison he beats Josefino and Bonifacia, but he accepts her new vocation as a whore. He and his friends begin to accept money from her in order to live.

Eventually, the novel asserts the primacy of the values of Anselmo, values which bring joy and love to Piura, over the values of the *caudillo*, Don Julio Reátegui. Don Julio, along with the power of the church, forces people out of the jungle and destroys the lives of those within the jungle. Anselmo loves Toñita and later loves giving his music, as a harpist, to the town.

Thirty years after the original Green House was burned down by Father García, Anselmo, an old man, dies, and, as might be expected, the people around him are as confused about the meaning of his life as they are about the way they are living their own lives. Chunga calls Dr. Zevallos, now an old man but at one time one of the most respectable patrons of the Green House, to attend to her father, Anselmo. She also calls for Father García, also an old man now. He is called the firebug among the people for having burned the original Green House. After the two men determine that Anselmo is indeed dead, Dr. Zevallos and Father García leave Chunga's place and Dr. Zevallos insists that they go have something hot, some kind of breakfast, at Angélica Mercedes' place. Father García reluctantly goes along in the taxi. The taxi driver predicts that the Mangaches, as the Black people in Piura are called, will make Anselmo, so well loved by them, into a saint, will "pray to him the way they do to Domitila, the holy woman" (384).

Angélica Mercedes, who as a young girl was present when Toñita, Anselmo's great love, died and Chunga was born, greets the two old men at her street cafe in Mangache and they tell her that Anselmo is dead. While she prepares their breakfast, Dr. Zevallos defends Anselmo, but Father García pounds the table; he will never accept the infamy of the relationship between Anselmo and Toñita. He believes the devil to be everywhere in Piura. Yet Anselmo's morality has taken over the city; Father García, thinks savagery has triumphed over civilization.

It is, evidently, time for judgment in the novel. Lituma, the former Sergeant, and Wildflower come in. Lituma continues to judge. He tells the priest that Chunga wants him, Father García, to say mass at Anselmo's funeral. Father García and Lituma get angry. Lituma calls the old priest a firebug for burning Anselmo's Green House. The two have a shouting confrontation and then the old priest gets an asthma attack, after which he falls asleep at his table. While he is asleep the others discuss the priest's lifelong hatred for Anselmo, and how although Anselmo had reason to hate Father García, he knew how to forgive while Father García did not.

The values of the jungle are shown to be superior to the values of the city. Bonifacia recalls that she was closer to Anselmo than anyone because they both came from the jungle. The narrative then moves back in time to a discussion between Anselmo and Bonifacia concerning the jungle:

"Really, Don Anselmo?" Wildflower asks. "You were born there too? Isn't it true
that the jungle's beautiful, with all the trees and all the birds? Isn't it true that people
are nicer back there?"

"People are the same everywhere, girl," the harpist says. "But it is true that the jungle
is beautiful. I've forgotten everything about what it's like there now, except for the color,
that's why I painted my harp green" (402).

Angélica decides they must go hire a priest, but Father García wakes
up and says that he will attend to the mass, that Chunga has asked
him. He and Dr. Zevallos leave to go home just as a taxi comes in,
accompanied by many people somewhat like a religious procession. The
taxi is bringing Anselmo's body to Angélica's for the wake. He has indeed
become a holy man for the poor people of Piura.

Don Julio Reátegui seems forgotten at the end of the novel, and
the two old men—attempting to assign guilt or innocence to Anselmo—
seem confused. This reader felt like an intruder, as if he had stumbled
into the midst of a group of people at an inopportune moment, a moment
of family grief. It takes conscious effort to recall that Wildflower, the
now aging whore, was once the innocent Bonifacia in Santa Maria de
Nieves, and that Lituma, the man who lives from the money his wife
makes as a whore, was once a decent man. Such a motley group of
characters, seen simultaneously, as Vargas Llosa presents them to us,
are like quaint snapshots taken on one's trip to an obscure Peruvian
city. But even as Vargas Llosa presents them as such, we know that
their lives have pattern, that the way they are has a cause. Life in Piura,
the life in and around the new Green House, appears to reflect the quaint
laziness and decadence of a group of social outcasts. *La Casa Verde*,
however, demonstrates that behind the sordid lives being lived out beneath
the corrugated iron roof of Chunga's whore house, as a causal agent
for the disordered lives of many of the inhabitants, exists a cultural
institution called *caudillaje* and a specific *caudillo*, Don Julio Reátegui.

The effort at ethical judgment in such a place among such people
reflects an effort to maintain standards for decent lives. Thus life in
Chunga's Green House represents an effort to impose order even among
people whose lives have been permanently disordered by the hard hand
of the *caudillo*.

Possession and Madness: El Señor Presidente

The institution of *caudillaje*, if one takes as evidence the work of
serious novelists, not only creates disorder when, according to popular
mythology it is supposed to create order, but also creates a world wherein
one's senses cannot be trusted, wherein truth is only the truth that the
caudillo perceives, wherein all reality becomes the reality of one
individual—the *caudillo*. While *Aquila Solitaria* and the novels of M.L.

Estefanía celebrate benevolent *caudillos* whose moral vision and power maintain justice, Miguel Angel Asturias *defamiliarizes* such a concept in his novel, *El Señor Presidente.*

Just as *Shane* shows the reader what it is like to live within the world of the cowboy hero on the frontier, *El Señor Presidente* shows the reader what it is like to live within the world of the *caudillo.* The *caudillo* in *El Señor Presidente,* for the people living beneath his rule, has divine power, and thus can alter and even create reality. Perhaps that is why novels about *caudillos* lend themselves to the technique made famous by other Latin American novelists, such as Gabriel Garcia Marquez and Mario Vargas Llosa, called *Magical Realism. Magical Realism* has been defined as a technique wherein "reality and fantasy are united in such a way that the line between the two worlds disappears...Both worlds are interrelated" (Arisso Thompson 112). The same scholar goes on to tell us the following: Each [one of the] points of view, is real for the individual, the combination of all of the parts [points of view] taken together is fantasy. One thus sees clearly that it is impossible to perceive the reality of the contemporary world in its totality, one may only appreciate something chaotic without sense nor logic" (Arisso Thompson, 114).

As may be seen in *La Casa Verde,* the reader can, with effort, perceive a totality and determine the causal relationship between events. However, in the world of the *caudillo,* since the world is an extension of his ego, only the *caudillo* can see the world immediately in its totality. He has power over life and death, he has power over economic welfare, he has power to allow happiness or to take away happiness and give misery. His power makes him terrifying in his wrath, and yet makes him the embodiment of benevolence when he is kind. This is not to suggest that Latin American people suffering under the rule of a *caudillo* worship idols. However, as may be seen in *El Señor Presidente,* the *caudillo* rules by imposing upon the superstition of the people and by presenting an aura of divinity and supernatural power. Therefore he becomes the center, to which all must turn before they can act.

El Señor Presidente is about the events that follow the killing of Colonel José Parrales Sonriente by the Zany, one of the poor, simple people who live under the cathedral porch in the capital of the city where the *caudillo*—the President—rules. The President claims that the death of Colonel Parrales Sonriente was associated with an attempt on his own life. He declares a national holiday in honor of his survival of what he tells the people was an assassination attempt by former close colleagues, General Canavales and the lawyer, Carvajal, two men who have fallen from his favor. Thus the death of Parrales Sonriente, caused almost by accident, simply because the Zany had been teased by other street people until he was driven to the mad act, becomes something else, an assassination attempt, decreed so by the *caudillo* for his own ends. Reality becomes whatever the *caudillo* creates. The *caudillo* becomes God.

On the national holiday in honor of the *caudillo's* survival, important people in their carriages follow the flag to the Palace. The language suggests that the President *is* God: "Señor! Señor! Heaven and earth are full of your glory" (96)! The narrator repeats this chant five times in two paragraphs. Since, in Spanish, the Lord is addressed as Señor, the narrator makes the connection between the Deity and the President explicit:

> "Señor! Señor! Heaven and earth are full of your glory! The women felt the divine power of their Beloved Deity. The more important priests paid him homage." (96)

The pronoun him, it should be emphasized, refers to the *caudillo,* not to God.

Angel Face, the President's handsome assistant, feeds the President's image of himself as God by comparing the ruler with Jesus in a *soto voc* compliment. The *caudillo* becomes, not like God, but actually God, the embodiment of the Deity on earth.

Since the *caudillo* is God, he can and does create reality in his domain. All reality becomes subject to the interpretation of the *caudillo*. As a result one thing can become another, fantasy can become reality, and reality can become fantasy. All things can become anything as the external world becomes totally subjective, i.e. the extension of the primary individual. The distortion of time and observable reality creates a world in which time loses past and future and becomes only the present time of the *caudillo*. Future plans are futile, and one's past, no matter how virtuous or vile, may be meaningless. Nothing in the observable world can be trusted to be what it appears to be and everything in the external world can become whatever the *caudillo* wants it to be. As a result the world becomes highly unpredictable. Truth can become a lie and a lie can become the truth.

Systems of justice, one assumes, search for truth. Yet when the Judge Advocate questions a woman, he assumes she is guilty and does not give her the opportunity to prove her innocence. Niña Fedina, the wife of Genaro Rodas, a man who is trying to get a job serving the President, was found at the home of General Canales the morning after the police attempted to arrest the General. Since the General had been warned he would be arrested, he had escaped, but Niña Fedina was not aware of that. She had discovered from her husband that an attempt would be made on the General's life. Because she had asked Camila, the General's daughter, to be the Godmother of her child, she felt an obligation to warn the girl. When she got to the house it was deserted. She went in to look for the young woman and, before she could leave, the police took her prisoner. The Judge Advocate refused to believe her when she told him she didn't know where the General was, which she didn't. After torture, after having her child die in her arms, she is sold to be made into a whore. The Judge Advocate knows that the reality, imposed by the President, demands that the General have associates, fellow traitors, and thus that not only the General, but others must also be guilty of an attempt on the life of the leader. Niña Fedina becomes a convenient part of that reality.

Thus, there can be a constant contrast between what the reader knows to be true and what is presented in the fiction. People perceive joy and happiness, but behind the walls of the prison a terrible reality exists. As the woman laments that her son is dying and pleads for the jailers to let her give the baby her milk, the national celebration for the survival of the President, with great festivities, goes on outside.

Reality crumbles in the madness of the country of the *caudillo*. Genaro Rodas, Niña Fedina's husband, sees his companion, Lucio Vasquez, a thug used by the *caudillo* to take care of minor dirty business, kills the Zany. Since the Zany was crazy he would not accept the *caudillo's* reality, which demanded that he be innocent of the crime he committed and that General Canales and the lawyer, Carvajal, be guilty. Therefore he had to be killed since he insisted on confessing to the crime.

Genaro, at home with his wife, extremely disturbed by the crime, officially sanctioned, even ordered, by the *caudillo*, suffers hallucinogenic visions. "An eye was travelling over the fingers of his right hand like the circle of light from an electric bulb. From the little finger to the middle finger, thence to the ring finger, from ring finger to index, from index to thumb. An eye...A single eye. He could feel it throbbing. He tried to crush it by closing his hand hard, till his nails sank into his flesh. But it was impossible" (57). Reality becomes fragmented perception; inanimate objects, or objects which have no will of their own, act as if they had volition. His eye becomes an object in itself, his fingers separate from his body, and he perceives them as parts of a fragmented world. The *caudillo* does not directly create Genaro's distorted vision, yet within his world where everything can become something else, in a world in which to confess to a crime becomes a crime, such a way of seeing becomes inevitable.

All things come to life in the fantasy world, the world that is but an extension of the President, of the fear he inspires in people, of the consciousness he so completely dominates. For example, as Don Miguel Angel Face, the President's most trusted, or so it would seem, adviser, tries to sleep, his consciousness, filled with fear, won't let him rest. He has helped Camila, the deposed General's daughter, without the President's blessings. At first he helped her simply because she was a defenseless young woman, but later he falls in love with her. Together they try to find one of her uncles to take her in and go about knocking on the doors of her relatives. As Don Miguel Angel Face tries to sleep his mind creates the following:

> "Stop! It's not a drum; it's a door echoing to a blow from a knocker shaped like a brass hand! The knocks penetrate into every corner of the intestinal silence of the house, like augers. Rat-tat-tat...The drum of the house. Every house has its door-drum to summon the people who are its life, and when it is shut it is as if they lived death...Rat-tat of the house...door...rat-tat of the house...the water in the fountain is all eyes when it hears the sound of the door-drum, and people say crossly to the servants: "Oh they're knocking!..." (178).

In the world of fantasy and terror created by the *caudillo*, objects take on life. Houses have 'intestinal' life, doors become drums, knockers become hands, water has eyes and ears and people only have ears for what they want to hear.

In such a world the only security can be in complete loyalty to the President, even if that means denying fundamental family ties as well as one's past and present actions. As in Vargas Llosa's *The Green House*, the *caudillo*, who should bring order to the country, brings disorder and chaos, even to the most intimate relationships. Eventually Don Miguel Angel Face sees Juan Canales, Camila's favorite uncle, the brother of General Canales. Miguel Angel Face wants Juan Canales to take General Canales' daughter, his niece, into his care, in short, to be a decent man and uncle. Juan Canales is terrified that any association with his brother or his brother's family will incriminate him. He sees Don Miguel Angel Face as an enemy spy sent by the President to link him to his brother's supposed crimes. He becomes completely undone.

> "The fact that he was innocent made no difference. How complicated it all was. How complicated!"
> It's a lottery, my friend, it's a lottery! It's a lottery, my friend, a lottery!"
> This phrase, describing the typical state of affairs in the country, used to be shouted by Old Fulgencio, a good old man who sold lottery tickets in the street, and was a devout Catholic with a sharp eye for business. Instead of Angel Face, Canales saw the skeleton silhouette of Old Fulgencio, whose bony limbs, jaws and fingers all seemed to be jerking on wires.
> Old Fulgencio used to...say in a voice which emerged simultaneously from his nose and his toothless mouth: "The lottery is the only law on this earth, my friend! The lottery can send you to prison, have you shot, make you a deputy, a diplomat, President of the Republic, a general or a minister! What's the good of work, when all this can be got by the lottery? It's a lottery, my friend—so come on and buy a lottery ticket!" (102)

In the magical world of the *caudillo*, one's behavior does not determine one's social or economic condition. In the terror filled world of the *caudillo*, the senses are not true measures of reality as people become deranged by fear and panic. As the lawyer Carvajal's wife races to the country home of the President to seek a pardon, her reality becomes totally subjective and deranged. The prose imitates her state of mind.

> "...yes she must save her husband...yes, yes, yes, yes, yes...her hair had come down—save him—her blouse came unfastened—save him. But the carriage wouldn't move...she could feel that it wasn't moving, only the front wheels were turning, she could feel the back wheels lagging behind so that the carriage was lengthening out like the bellows of a camera, and she could see the horses getting smaller and smaller in the distance." (216)

Once at the *caudillo's* country estate she is not allowed to enter. Her husband is executed.

Don Miguel Angel Face eventually marries Camila, without the President's knowledge or blessing. In short, he tries to create a reality beyond that of the *caudillo*. It is a tremendous risk, since not only is he giving shelter to the daughter of a man who has become known, through the magic of the President's abuse of reality, as a criminal, but he has also simply acted in his own stead, as an independent individual, and in the world of the *caudillo*, who possesses all, such action is intolerable, especially by a man he possesses in a confidential, relationship. Don Miguel Angel Face is called to the office of the President. As he talks with the President for what turns out to be the last time, and just after it appears that his salvation is at hand when the President apparently awards him the post of Ambassador to the United States, he too suffers from a state of altered perception. He sees mythological figures which dance before the god of fire, Tohil. It is the reality of Don Miguel Angel Face's mind, perhaps dominated by myths unconsciously known, but since it takes place under the psychological condition of terror imposed by the *caudillo*, the *caudillo* can be said to have caused it.

The world surrounding the *caudillo* becomes an extension of his own person, and the world becomes a reflection of his own condition. In the President's prison four men talk. One is a sacristan who, unable to read, unfortunately removed the announcement of the birthday of the President's mother from the church door instead of the notice of the Virgin of La O's novena, which he had been told to remove. His mistake has cost him an indeterminate prison sentence. Another is the lawyer, Carvajal, who was arrested the day the police tried to arrest General Canales. Another prisoner is a student, presumably a Leftist. The fourth prisoner speaks.

> The fourth voice murmured faintly: "There's no hope of freedom for us, my friends; we must put up with this as long as God wills. The men of this town who desired their country's good are far away now: some of them begging outside houses in a foreign land, others rotting in a common grave. A day will come when no one dares walk the streets of this town. Already the trees don't bear fruit as they used to. Maize is less nourishing

than it was. Sleep is less restful; water is less refreshing. The air is becoming impossible to breathe. Plagues follow epidemics, epidemics follow plagues, and soon an earthquake will put an end to us all. My eyes tell me that our race is doomed! When it thunders, it is a voice from heaven crying: 'You are evil and corrupt, you are accomplices in wickedness!' Hundreds of men have had their brains blown out against our prison walls by murderous bullets. Our marble palaces are wet with innocent blood. Where can one turn one's eyes in search of freedom!'" (201)

The land has come to life—or rather death; the President's moral decay, and the sterile terror he imposes, has created a decaying world, a world without life. The President *is* the country. As both God and country, the President becomes all reality. Still, just as with the concept of country, and the reality of God, the individual frequently finds the *caudillo* difficult to locate in the sensory world.

It is no doubt appropriate, therefore, that the reader does not actually meet the President—hear him speak, read a description, until page 220, Chapter XXXII, "The President." Angel Face is going to see the President for the last time, when he has the mythical vision after having been told that he was to become Ambassador to the United States. He goes into the room. When he does so, "The President advanced from the far end of the room; the ground seemed to advance under his feet and the house over his head" (221). Thus when the President moves the world moves. The *caudillo's* person becomes the body of the world.

In the disordered and squalid frontier world of Vargas Llosa's *The Green House*, readers see what becomes of lives lived where a *caudillo* has the power to destroy personal and public order and personal and public morality. In the terrifying world of Asturias' *El Señor Presidente* we see how the *caudillo* subsumes all reality, how he possesses all reality, how his personality becomes the only personality of the country he dominates.

The Source of Power: Language in Las tierras flacas

In the final novel to be considered in this chapter, *Las tierras flacas*, *[The Lean Lands]*, Agustin Yáñez presents a more positive view of the relationship between rural Mexican people and the strong men that sometimes rule them, the *caudillos* or, in this case, the *caciques*. In *Las tierras flacas* one may see how the *cacique*, the small town *caudillo*, enforces his rule but cannot enforce permanent change upon a village. *Las tierras flacas* demonstrates how the *cacique* uses traditional, conservative wisdom of the community in order to dominate, much as popular writers use traditional, conservative audience ideology to assure large sales of their books. But in spite of the *caciques'* efforts to change people, to exploit them or to bring them material progress, that very traditionalism, that very conservatism, prevails to maintain a culture that maintains its integrity, a culture that accepts and adapts to superficial change without permanent damage to the dignity and morality of the people.

Plot is very important in Yáñez's novel, which when abbreviated seems very like allegory—like a *Pilgrim's Progress* for the *cacique*. Indeed, Matiana, the village seer, healer, and religious leader, judges the triumph of Jacob Gallo—the new *cacique* at the end of the fiction—as hollow, since he has stepped from the straight and narrow path.

As the novel begins Epifanio Trujillo is the *cacique* of the area called the *Tierra Santa*, the Holy Lands. He began as a poor man but decided early to establish a Trujillo dynasty. To do so he has sired many children with many concubines, although he has never married. Rómulo, a poor farmer, the grandson of the former strong man, Teódulo, is in desperate financial condition as the story begins. Epifanio tricked Rómulo's father and uncles out of their inheritance and Rómulo has been reduced to borrowing from the *cacique*. His daughter, Teófila, a lovely and somehow educated young woman who studied and lived away from the village for a time, knows how to sew. Upon her return to her parent's home, with borrowed money, Rómulo bought her a sewing machine. She read scripture to all the village, taught, and behaved like a saint. Epifanio paid court to the young girl but before he could work his wicked will she died of meningitis. Teófila, it is thought by the community, is a saint, and her sewing machine, kept in perfect condition by her mother, Merced, becomes a sacred relic.

Epifanio, convinced that he has lost his one true love when Teófila died, wants her sewing machine as a remembrance. Of course, Merced, Rómulo's wife, wants to keep the machine, as does Rómulo, but Epifanio demands either the machine or Rómulo's land—mortgaged to Epifanio.

However, Epifanio himself is not in perfect condition. Fat and old, he can barely fit into a chair. He eats all of the time, and the only one that can control him at all is Plácida, his oldest daughter, a sharp tongued shrew. Moreover, Miguel Arcángel, his oldest son, who Epifanio tried to punish by taking away his authority as oldest son when he married—without Epifanio's approval—a young woman who Epifanio himself fancied, has returned to challenge his father's rule. When his father tried to punish him, some twenty years before the novel begins, Miguel Arcángel, rather than accept the punishment, took his new wife and his mother and ran away to the United States. He has returned in a position of authority, as commissary, and with money. Having changed his name to Jacob Gallo, he has renounced the name of Trujillo, thus totally alienating his father.

Jacob Gallo, formerly Miguel Arcángel, wants progress. He introduces irrigation, modern farming methods, even a barometer for predicting the weather, techniques he has learned in the United States. He causes—or at least his return coincides—with an enormous event:

an airplane flies over the land, which most of the village people think is the devil. Soon Jacob Gallo begins to rival his father, becoming the new *cacique*.

Meanwhile, Felipe, Jesusito, and Plácida, still loyal to their father, Epifanio, begin to fight over power within their father's domain as his strength and force diminishes. Jesusito and Felipe quarrel violently after Jesusito, in an effort to ingratiate himself with his father, goes to Rómulo's farm and takes Teófila's sacred sewing machine. After Felipe and Jesusito fight, Jesusito retires to his own ranch to connive and Felipe does the same, taking the sewing machine with him, since he is the strongest. Plácida begins to take over the big farm.

On a very eventful day on which Jacob Gallo predicted rain would finally come to the land after a dry spring, as the rain does actually come, along with thunder and much portentous activity by the male animals who sense the storm, the old *cacique*, Epifanio, dies of a heart attack.

Jesusito and Felipe want the money and power their sister controls. When Matiana, the holy woman, goes to see Plácida to try to get the sewing machine back (she thinks Plácida has it), she is set upon by Jesusito's thugs who claw her eyes out. Jesusito planned the attack in order to make Plácida look guilty and cause people to turn against her. Enraged, the village people do more than turn against Plácida. They go to Felipe's ranch, hang him, return the sewing machine to Merced, then go to the big ranch, dig up the body of Epifanio, burn the house, and leave Plácida destitute. Finally they go to the ranch of Jesusito but he manages to escape. Jacob Gallo, the new *cacique*, restores order, but it is a military order, and it cannot, according to Matiana, be sustained. A new order, more legal, perhaps, has been established, but it too will fall, just as the former *caciques* have fallen, like Rómulo's grandfather and like Epifanio. The people of the *Tierra Santa* cannot escape the endless repetition of rule by a strong man, a *cacique*, but the *caciques* cannot cause permanent change to the people of the *Tierra Santa*.

The first Spanish dictionary of the Academy, published in 1729 defined the *cacique* as the most energetic—sometimes the most violent— who became "the first of his village or the republic, the one who has more authority or power and who because of his pride wants to make himself feared and obeyed by all his inferiors" (Chevalier 39). To be the most powerful, one must influence people and gain respect. To be sure, in novels such as *Recurso al metodo [Return to the Method]* and *El Señor Presidente,* readers are shown that, once in power, *caudillos* must be willing to be ruthless, cruel, absolutely without mercy, that the method for obtaining and sustaining power requires sadism beyond measure. But at a more intimate psychological level, prior to obtaining absolute power that enables such demonstrations, the individual must be able to make people believe that he or she has special abilities and special knowledge.

Agustin Yáñez, in *Las tierras flacas,* demonstrates how a strong man uses the wisdom of the community in order to dominate the minds of the people and thereby gain the special power of the *cacique.* Proverbs and/or sayings, terse and epigrammatic, encapsulate the wisdom of a community. Those who can use them dominate communal wisdom, especially among non-literate people who do not have access to the written word. Proverbs, like an image, have a sense of finality, of closure; they preclude debate and discussion. The only response to a proverb is another proverb. If a new job, one with a potential for gain or loss, appears, one's friends or spouse might counsel, if they favor the change: "Nothing ventured; nothing gained." But if they favor security, they might well say, "A bird in the hand is worth two in the bush." One proverb answers the other; both preclude words based upon observation and reason.

Proverbs, like the images from television and film, are known and shared by those within a particular language and cultural domain. In *Las tierras flacas,* Epifanio Trujillo dominates because he dominates proverbial, communal knowledge and wisdom. Even when the old *cacique* is so fat that he must struggle for breath and his double chin pulls his mouth down making it hard for him to speak, "Popular sayings, which he uses maliciously, are never off his lips" (35). In fact, when meditating later on, he acknowledges that he needs such sayings "in order to feel alive the way you need air to breath" (110).

Eventually, as his strength fails him, Epifanio suffers rebellion within his huge family. He refuses to allow the village Christmas pageantry to be staged at his home, the Big House, called Belén. For self-serving ends, Plácida, Jesusito, and Felipe want to have the pageantry, traditionally held at the big house, staged there as it has been in the past for as long as anyone can remember. They confront the old, fat man, who, at first, "showed sign of giving in. Then he started off again, entering into an interminable duel of old sayings with his sons.

"Time is a good counselor and will reveal the truth...Since the atole's mine, I'll stir it with my own stick...Some hens do a lot of crackling and never lay an egg...The man who's really a man doesn't look for a boost...Don't let yourself get hurt and make matters worse..." (114)

Surprisingly, Epifanio eventually allows the mummery to be held at his home, primarily because Jesusito appeals to his greed by suggesting that they charge the vendors who sell at the annual event a fee for the right to set up their stands.

Epifanio was able to dominate because he knew the heart of the community, the sayings, which gave him power. As he defends himself after his death before the accusing angel he notes, "How were they [others in the community] going to catch me in their trap if they couldn't even get ahead of me in sayings" (254)!

Others also use proverbs in order to think and to communicate. Rómulo's grandfather, Teódulo, the *cacique* who preceded Epifanio, has access to such wisdom. "Working with debt hanging over your head is like trying to carry water in a basket" (12), he tells his grandson.

The sayings, which conserve tradition and oppose innovation, reflect the fundamental conservatism of the community. Rómulo's grandfather not only conserved the traditional wisdom in sayings, he was also conservative in sexual and financial matters. He thinks that those who go about looking for buried treasure are foolish, just as those who go to other villages, who envy what others in other communities might have, are traitors and fools (12). People only leave "out of stupidity, curiosity, and evil desires" (20). Teódulo distrusted change of any kind. When Rómulo's friend, Palemón, who has already been in contact with Jacob Gallo, urges Rómulo to try to remember where his Grandfather might have hidden money, or where his Grandfather might have known of minerals that could be mined, Rómulo recalls his grandfather's words: "There's gold here, and who knows what other metals, but woe to the man who tries to mine them because they'll bring unhappiness to these farms and an endless chain of disasters" (22). When Palemón tells Rómulo that some men want to use divining rods to discover water—the men are working with Jacob Gallo—Rómulo is very reluctant. He is afraid of getting mixed up with strangers (25).

The entire village distrusts strangers as well as those who have had undue contact with strangers, just as in the world of *Aquila Solitaria* or in the comics of Rius. Epifanio, eager to discredit Jacob Gallo, starts rumors that Gallo's powers are not technology but the result of a pact with Satan. Then the season begins without rain and it looks as if there will be a drought. "The farmers stood gazing and thought to themselves that there must be some truth in the rumors about the pact with the devil, about the King of Diamond's [Jacob Gallo] being a Protestant and getting money from the Masons" (221). Obviously anyone who had been in contact with a Protestant or a Mason would have been in contact with a stranger.

People begin to pray for rain. Jacob Gallo predicts that it will rain on or before May 31. Nevertheless, people are more and more certain that the intruder, the person who has crossed the frontier, Jacob Gallo, has brought back with him moral and religious contamination.

Dominated by a way of knowing that transcends time, i.e. by means of sayings that are timeless in nature, and dominated by a sense that contact with strangers leads to troublesome change, the village people live outside time. Nevertheless, we are given an approximation of the time the fiction represents—sometime in the late 1920s. Matiana, we are told, was born the year the United States stole a large amount of land, which would be in 1847, at the conclusion of the war with Mexico when the United States annexed one third of the country (161). Matiana is eighty years old at the time of the fiction, so we can guess the time represented in the fiction as 1927. The information allows the reader, accustomed to diachronic ways of knowing, to locate himself in time. It does not change the synchronic world of the village.

Rómulo, in particular, cannot escape time. He constantly recalls the past, what his Grandfather, Teódulo said, or what had happened at such and such a time. As Merced, his wife, thinks: "Listening to the same old story all one's life—there's no escape till we die. All we can do is fold our arms, waiting patiently for God's will to be done" (102). As might be expected, during the majority of the fiction the characters, and the reader, are outside time. Matiana, who speaks for the community, and who, as seer and healer and village elder, knows all and sees all and has the final judgment for the reader in the novel, tells us: "How the time passes and the years come around, bringing the same dates and feast days, the same movements of the sun, moon, and stars. Nothing is changed, nothing that happens to the people can change the onset of the rainy season and its end, the coming of the cold weather and the warm weather, wind, clouds, hailstorms, long and short days, mornings, afternoons, nights, as the daily round continues throughout every season of the year... How time passes and nothing changes in the life of the countryside, with its annual cycle of seed-time and harvest, endlessly repeated and accepted, year after year, day after day..." (79-80).

Outside time, in the traditional world of the community, private property does not exist. In the communal world ruled by Rómulo's grandfather, all things, as Rómulo recalls, were shared. Private property was communal property. Since Rómulo provides a voice for what one must consider the *norm* for village thought, his judgments can be taken as reflections of the thought of the most traditional of the people in the village. With the advent of the 1910 Mexican revolution, the concept of private property came under considerable criticism. Redistribution of the land was a primary concern. It was, in fact, the only area of economic life in which socialism had existed *prior* to the revolution. As one historian notes, "Socialism, however, was not rooted in the Mexican economic order *except* [my italics] in the system of the *ejido*, or rural communal property, which had existed during the colonial epoch as a Spanish system imposed on an Aztec tradition..." (Henriquez Ureña 99). With the coming of the revolution, it was politically appropriate that Rómulo should look back to a time—and a place—isolated from governments which sustained the idea of private property, when communal property was the rule, as during the time of his grandfather, Teódulo.

However, Epifanio Trujillo, the old, fat and decadent *cacique,* and Jacob Gallo, the new, young, and innovative *cacique,* try to change *Tierra Santa.* Epifanio imposes a new order, not entirely in the best interest of the people of the area. His changes emphasize the concept of private property. Rómulo recalls: "Envy began when Pifanio [Epifanio] started to thrive, to be harsh toward others, refusing to lend remedies for the sick—the enema apparatus, laxatives, medicinal herbs. The bad example spread" (153).

The concept of private property is alien to the village. When Epifanio allows Felipe, Plácida, and Jesusito to have the Christmas pastorals at the big house, at Belén, and they charge the vendors for space, the community is very angry. One person says: "They think they own even the air and the sun and the stars. Didn't they want to make us pay for the moonlight" (144)? When Felipe tries to collect he uses a pistol and smashes one man's guitar over the man's head. There is a general riot. Jesusito answers one village person who asks, "By what right?" with: "This is a private house, not a public square. How can you expect to take all the profit without contributing to the cost? It isn't fair" (149). In other words, he claims the law of private property in a community that has been accustomed to communal property. When things continue to go badly, the Trujillos accuse the peddlers of selling bad goods, bad food, of giving short measure, and so forth. Finally, Jesusito says:

"Then let them get out of the patio, carry on their trading outside of our boundaries."
"And who knows," asked the leader from Betulia, "where your boundaries are?"
There were smiles all around, either open or concealed.
Don Felipe started to attack the questioner. Don Jesusito held him back.
"Did I say something I shouldn't? Was I impolite? According to you, everything is yours. Just tell us where. That's all I want to know, in order to avoid further trouble." (151)

Epifanio Trujillo's innovations were, he claims as he defends himself on the day of his death, not all bad for the community. However, it appears that his major innovation was the concept of private property, one which he used in order to exploit the village people.

Jacob Gallo also tries to innovate, apparently with the good of the community in mind. When asked by Jesusito what he intends to do with his authority and his police, Jacob answers: "Establish order and justice. Security..." (184). He offers the community progress, new systems for making the land more productive, changes brought from the United States. "If they [Jesusito, Felipe, and Placida Trujillo] decided to become allies, the Trujillos would have these advantages: Jacob's help in settling the matter of their heritage and in modernizing their methods of agriculture; access to new techniques and products, among which Jacob mentioned reforestation, soil conservation, introduction of new crops, perforation of wells, construction of dams, opening up of roads, agriculture in place of cattle-raising, a variety of money crops, use of fertilizers, improved seeds and machinery; industrialization, exploitation of the forests in the Cardos mountains, investigation of the mining possibilities in the region; political power and influence, money and financial credit" (120-121). Jacob introduces irrigation on his own farm, and many of the other farmers copy his methods. He also finds a well on Rómulo's land, and, at the end of the fiction, introduces electricity to the village, installing it with elaborate ceremony on his own farm for the purpose of irrigation.

Nevertheless, whether the *caciques* are good, like Rómulo's grandfather, Teódulo and Jacob, or bad, like Epifanio, the village does not change. The village culture is impervious to change. The changes brought about by the return of Jacob Gallo are, ironically, attributed to the miraculous intervention of Teófila through the medium of her holy relic, the sewing machine. The year turns out to be an exceptionally good crop year. As people listen to the corn grow, however, they do not attribute it to Jacob Gallo's miracles, but to the miracles of the sewing machine, Teófila's relic (291). When Jacob Gallo's men discover a well on Rómulo's land, he thinks it is a Teófila miracle (231).

In order to assure permanent order after the *campesinos* have killed Felipe and destroyed the Big House, Jacob calls in soldiers. It is the first time as far as anyone knows that soldiers have come to *Tierra Santa*. It creates quite a sensation. Jacob proceeds to enforce order in the traditional ways of the *caudillo*. The spies caught inside Torres de San Miguel, Jacob Gallo's farm, are shot—presumably while trying to escape—as are those who put out Matiana's eyes. Their bodies are taken around tied on their horses as an exhibit, a lesson, to the village people. The families of the other prisoners, many who were villagers who acted in outrage, are worried. Jacob Gallo "went around raising hopes, bargaining and earning gratitude so that the whole neighborhood would feel itself under an obligation to him for the favor of his indulgence. Unwillingly, he started setting the prisoners free. But these and their families had already struck a bargain with the miraculous Machine, and they attributed to a miracle of the Machine the favor of their liberty" (314).

Merced, Rómulo's wife, speaks for many in the community as she deciphers events. She thinks that Matiana's sacrifice moved the sacred relic (the sewing machine) consecrated by Teófila, to cause the people to rid the land of the Trujillos. The change is not attributed to Jacob Gallo or his technology. In fact, Merced judges the new technology as lacking, as bringing with it the soldiers, a scourge the *Tierra Santa* will never get rid of. Jacob Gallo is merely a new *cacique,* a new iron fisted ruler, according to Merced (314-315).

Matiana reinforces Merced's judgment. After Plácida's home is burned by the angry village people, and after a suitable length of time for contemplation, Plácida goes to Matiana and throws herself at her feet, promising to serve her for the rest of her life. She is repentant. Plácida's conversion to the service of Matiana is attributed, by the people, to Teófila's machine. (323)

Less directly, the novel deprecates the changes brought about by Epifanio, his efforts to establish a dynasty through concubinage as well as his efforts to establish and maintain private property. Epifanio assumes absolute power and possession of the women and children in his huge family, just as he assumes absolute power and possession over the cattle on his ranch. He feels that he "was invested with undisputed authority in matters concerning his family" (37). After the birth of a child, he follows the progress of the mother and child much as a cattle rancher would follow the progress of a cow and her new calf. "He would watch over mother and child during the nursing period. He noted carefully the progressive manifestations of instincts and temperaments, the baby's way of sucking, crying, smiling, and taking notice; observed how the infants stood the teething period, the summer heat, the cold; observed their precocity or tardiness in crawling, standing, walking, running, talking, beginning to think. He graded them according to almost the same procedures as he used for the offspring of his favorite animals" (39).

Yet, as Merced notes, Epifanio's treatment of women was not really innovative. She laments that all of the people of *Tierra Santa* simply accept their fate without ever questioning it or trying to change. Women are especially susceptible. They are, and always have been, chattel, and their condition never changes. According to Merced, "We're only saucepans or metates to serve them. Like slaves. Before, we didn't rebel. We would if we weren't accustomed to endure, like animals who can't even kick" (104).

Epifanio tried to enforce the idea of private property. Yet, when he and his three greedy children push the concept too far they incite revolt. Since Julio Gallo says that he will only charge 8% interest for farm loans, and will forego many of the worst practices Epifanio has initiated, the reader can hope that the village will return to standards closer to those maintained by Teódulo in reference to property.

Both *caciques,* the bad and the good, the old and the new, think they have brought change to *Tierra Santa.* The new *cacique,* Julio Gallo, introduces many changes in agricultural techniques—already mentioned—and even electricity. The word, *progress,* becomes used often among people who follow Jacob. Yet, Matiana, the final judge for the community, sees his progress as ephemeral, his changes as no more lasting than those of Epifanio. In a timeless world innovations such as electricity cannot impose a new temporality. She compares Jacob Gallo's lightning rods to the change when petroleum lanterns began to take the "place of sticks of pitch pine and the wax and tallow candles used on the farms for light. When this dirty, smelly liquid made its first appearance. When they brought lamps and wicks and other things that made the people afraid since they believed they were works of the devil" (276). And, she notes, there were many accidents, including one in which many people were killed.

Matiana is the judge of the community. She metes out justice. It is supernatural, yet very closely linked to the earth and the values of the community (76). "Having no priests, no doctors, no judges, no police, what would the plain and the harsh country around it do without Matiana, the miracle worker? Her service is manifold: she has the gifts of a prophetess and exorcist, defender, chastiser, healer, adviser, comforter, and midwife, and can perform the burial rites. In public and private disasters, in this land of huisache and cactus" (78).

After Jacob Gallo has firmly established his new order, bringing progress along with soldiers and guns, Matiana judges him: "From now on he'll only be able to keep his position by force of arms, by terror, just building on sand the way the Trujillos did. All his money, all his cunning won't help. Life is like this, no one learns from his own experience. One evil goes and another comes. After the Trujillos, the Gallos. Poor Miguel Arcangel! He's not a bad man, but he took the downward road and strayed from the straight and narrow path" (321).

Matiana repeats her judgment of the new *cacique,* Jacob Gallo, when she takes the gold coins back to him with which he has tried to win her favor. She also repeats the Biblical saying, surely a part of village wisdom, as she says: "Take it, Miguel Arcangel, take this that I never accepted from you, that you have always refused to take back. I have made this journey with great sacrifice to hand it back to you, and to remind you that the higher you rise the greater your fall will be. There are no short cuts in the straight and narrow path" (327). She does this during the ceremony of the electricity on Jacob's farm, just as the new electric generator starts and a string of light bulbs come on, just as Jacob Gallo proclaims with pompous vacuity: "I like to do things on a big scale..." (328). The judgment seems clear. Jacob Gallo will cause no greater change in *Tierra Santa* than his father caused. His life will be just as futile.

In the critiques of *caudillaje,* the four major artists considered in this chapter condemn various elements of the system of government. Sarmiento attacks *caudillaje* because it thwarts civilization, because it kept Argentina from progressing with the rest of the world. To be sure, he also condemned the brutality and cruelty of the *caudillos.* Asturias creates a fictional world in which one senses that nothing that anyone, even the least substantial or unknown citizen does, can escape the omniscient eye of the *caudillo.* Asturias' novel depicts a world in which it seems as if the *caudillo* has indeed become a cruel God who rules with guile and betrays all who offer him their loyalty. Vargas Llosa lets us stop by a cheap bar and whore house, stop in as if we had simply decided, on a whim, to buy a cold beer, and while there, learn of the terrible disorder a *caudillo* can bring to a people. Finally, Yañez shows us how a community seems bound to suffer the domination of a strong man, yet, with a strength that goes far beyond politics, endures and maintains a culture that the *caciques* cannot touch.

Serious fictional studies of *caudillaje,* the traditional means for bringing order to the hinterlands, in conjunction with studies of popular celebrations of *caudillaje,* such as one finds in the novels of Estefanía and the comic books of *Aquila Solitaria,* demonstrate that Latin America seems to be doomed to constantly vacillate between subjugation to the power of one man and revolt against that power, only to be subjected again to the power of a new *caudillo.* Latin American old stories, and therefore Latin American culture, demand power and strength from leaders, and some of those leaders become *caudillos* and assume power only God should have. As long as the old stories prevail—and the culture accepts such power as necessary for order and decency and conservation of values—then *caudillos* will exist. If the stories which attempt to examine the reductions of popular narratives and images, stories such as those by Sarmiento, Asturias, Vargas Llosa and Yañez, should ever have the power to change the cultural phenomena they so skillfully critique, then Latin America could escape time and isolation and become a vibrant part of the rest of the world.

Chapter VIII
Conclusion

Probably no single cause can account for *caudillaje*. A widespread cultural characteristic, it seems to crop out in almost all parts of Latin America from time to time. However, it seems probable that a form of egocentrism that creates a personal sense of responsibility for all of one's family or community, a characteristic that can create warm and lasting friendships and enable people to truly care for one another, combined with great value for the conservation of tradition, inspires a few—extremists to be sure—to seek to dominate all of the people around them, to not only care for all those around them, but in a sense to possess all those around them, and eventually to possess their village and their country. Acknowledgement of such egocentrism as normal, as a means for the expression of the way people relate to one another, allows many people to accept the system of government called *caudillaje,* to accept possession and dominance for the sake of orderly lives and the sense that someone in power cares about their welfare and their way of life. People want to be cared about. People want their traditional order conserved. They seem to find the caring and the strength to conserve that order in a local or regional strong man, a *caudillo* or a *cacique.*

In the system of *caudillaje* the stability of the government depends upon the force of the *caudillo's* personality; in a sense, governmental stability depends upon the capacity of the *caudillo's* ego. If the *caudillo* leaves or loses his power, the order he has imposed seems to go with him. Since one man, the *caudillo,* holds all power and thereby provides all order, all men must look to the center of the government, the *caudillo,* for laws, for a sense of nation, for the strength to maintain government. The center of the government, the *caudillo,* becomes the center of the world. Perhaps this is one reason Latin Americans like popular narratives that inculcate a sense of distrust concerning frontiers. Perhaps this is one reason Latin Americans look toward the center, not toward hinterlands, for civilizing power. But since *caudillos* far too often care only for power, for dominance and possession and the expression of ego, the system of *caudillaje* far too often leads to the complete loss of human rights.

159

Unfortunately, mass literacy and modern means of communication have tended to conserve old ways of the imagination. The *cacique* was a part of the culture of Latin America in pre-Columbian times. *Caudillaje* became fundamental to the maintenance of order in Latin America hinterlands after the discovery and conquest. An institution so fundamental to a culture has not disappeared with time and education. In fact, time and education have made literature, in print and through electronic means, available to many more people than in the days of illiteracy and isolation. Today comic books are the everyday reading of the vast majority of Latin American people. In Mexico, "Estimates for total production of comic books and photonovels...in the early 1980s suggest that 100 million copies are sold each month, or more than 1 billion annually" (Hinds 24)! Along with comic books, Latin Americans read enormous numbers of novels by authors such as M.L. Estefanía. Such familiar, seemingly innocent literature—and the images it sustains— affirms traditional ideology and faith in leaders, *caudillos* or *caciques*, who personify government and order.

In Anglo America the Europeans who eventually dominated the continent—indeed, the hemisphere—brought with them from Europe a sense that men who had found salvation had been given divine instruction to cultivate the soil in an orderly fashion. Anglo Americans believed that to colonize land in order to till it properly, to make it more productive and to be good stewards of God's gifts would win redemption. Moreover, ownership of land meant freedom and independence. As colonists, they wanted someone to help them establish themselves on the land, and if that took violent means then they wanted someone proficient in violence. They did not want, however, to submit to such a man forever; in many cases they had left Europe to escape such domination. Therefore, they imagined a frontiersman who would establish order and then move on, and in imagining such a hero they imagined an ever-expanding frontier, one which would take them to all the land not populated by men like themselves. They imagined the frontiersman, later to become the cowboy, a nomadic man of violence who, given his nature, would remain loyal to Anglo American culture while venturing ever into land which he would pacify in order to make way for liberty, democracy, and the colonists.

Anglo Americans also brought with them from Europe a sense of the hierarchy of the races. The White race was preeminent. The Black race was at the bottom end of the scale. Native Americans were not white and obviously inferior. Latin Americans, darker skinned than Anglo American, and guilty—from an Anglo American point of view—of miscegenation with Native Americans, were also inferior. Moreover, like Native Americans, Latin American people appeared to have been unsuccessful in making their land rich. Even today, as they struggle with huge national debts and frightful individual poverty, it seems apparent to many that Latin American people need the superior model offered by the United States, a model which, some feel, should be imposed if they are unwilling to accept it along with financial aid and dependency.

Given Anglo American frontier ideology it is natural to think of Latin Americans as not among God's chosen people (Zea 219-220). Indeed, it became fashionable very early in the history of the United States to think of Latin Americans in racist stereotypes which justified expansionism. To offer Latin Americans the opportunity for democratic order, and to teach Latin American people how to do business the Anglo American way, seems to many, still, to be nothing less than the duty of the United States. To protect them from the excesses of their foolish revolutions, so frequently radical in the twentieth-century, seems but a logical extension of the protection and developmental opportunities the United States feels justified and obligated to offer. Just as it was once the Manifest Destiny to bring salvation to the Native American's land, so it now seems manifest to many that it is Anglo America's duty to teach Latin Americans to govern themselves according to the model provided by the United States in order to be successful.

Americans, according to President Truman, "had an obligation to maintain an international environment open to 'free institutions, representative government, free elections, guarantees of individual liberty, freedom of speech, religion, and freedom from political oppression' '' (Hunt 158). The icon of the cowboy perfectly conveyed this idea—the cowboy who made the world safe for settlers, for colonists, the cowboy who policed the uncivilized parts of the world or uncivilized behavior in civilized parts of the world. The ideas are as old as Thomas Jefferson and Henry Adams, and as new as Louis L'Amour and George Bush.

Just as in Latin America, mass literacy and technology maintain traditional frontier ideology in the United States. Louis L'Amour's novels promote the idea that the destiny of the Anglo American must be to establish order, and that older forms of civilization, such as Latin American civilizations, must give way before the march of progress. Gene Autry reinforced for an entire generation a pattern deeply embedded in the culture of the United States, that where disorder and confusion prevail, it is the proper role of the hero from the United States to set things right, with or without legal sanction. To proselytize for the American Way of Life isn't just good business; it is a cultural imperative based in religion, a self-righteous sense of duty, and in deeply ingrained racism which tells the Anglo American that he must impose his will upon people who are not really capable of choosing for themselves.

Serious artists have examined, used and attempted to *defamiliarize* the ideology inherent in the icon of the cowboy. Walter Van Tilburg Clark, in *The Ox-Bow Incident*, demonstrated how the self-righteous morality communicated by the Western can lead to the miscarriage of justice, indeed, to attitudes which he associated with Fascist governments. E.L. Doctorow, in *Welcome to Hard Times,* tested the idea of town building, inherent in the Western from its inception, an optimistic vision of how Anglo American social and political structures can and should be imposed as a means of bringing order to savage lands. He also asked his readers to examine the assumption in Westerns, and a part of the optimistic view of Anglo Americans, that one can always, in the words of Thomas Paine, "begin the world all over again" (Hunt 19). The world, Doctorow concluded, was not as benign as the Western, and the ideology therein, would have us believe. Thomas Berger, in *Little Big Man,* questions the cheerful reliance upon rationalism the Western advocates. Jack Schaefer, in *Shane,* poignantly showed how the Western has sustained a divided image for manhood and proper behavior, an image which, on the one hand, would have us venturing to foreign lands to make the whole world over in our own image while, on the other hand, would have us perfect the space we already have, and the liberty therein.

Each of the serious Western novelists examined in this book has demonstrated that the pattern for thought provided by the Western can damage people, even though such heroes, in the world of the imagination, bring order that enables colonization. By examining the psychological, philosophic and social impact of the cowboy as hero in Anglo America, such novels show us that we must think carefully about our heroes, about what kind of men they should be, whether they should be men of peace or men of war. They ask us to question whether our expansive optimism and our self-righteous sense that our way of doing things, of governing ourselves and dividing our goods, are the only possible patterns for a civilization.

Serious artists have also examined the phenomenon of the *caudillo* and have attempted to *defamiliarize* the preferred frontier ideology of Latin America. Domingo Sarmiento bitterly denounced the personalism, the egoism, which he felt Rosas and Facundo exemplified. Miguel Angel Asturias showed readers how terror can and does alter phenomenon in a world where only one reality, that of the *caudillo,* exists. In his narrative he demonstrated how the *caudillo* becomes associated by the people with the Messiah, an idea which Mario Vargas Llosa explored in *La guerra del fin del mundo* (1981), in which the *caudillo,* without political portfolio, was a religious fanatic who possessed his followers because they believed in him as the Messiah. We have seen in *La casa verde,* by that same brilliant Peruvian novelist, how domination by a *caudillo* created terrible disorder on a frontier in Peru among a group of people ultimately lost in the backwash of time and space.

Agustin Yáñez's novel, *Las tierras flacas,* about life in a small, remote village of Jalisco, Mexico, just after the twentieth-century revolution, shows how the *cacique* obtains power through the force of his personality and dominance of the reductive imagery inherent in proverbs. His novel also demonstrates the strength of communal culture, the resistance to change in such culture, and how that is both its great strength and its great weakness.

Serious novels soon become standard on reading lists for high school and university students. This assures them places in literary histories and critical studies. It does not assure that they will have much impact outside the classroom unless teachers are able to see how they comment upon cultural patterns which affect human behavior. Along with the novels labeled serious, the narratives people actually read and watch must also be scrutinized in classrooms in order to teach students that the seemingly innocent world of popular literature can inculcate and reinforce ideology that may or may not provide us with the best of all patterns for judging how to behave in the world. Whether traditional ways of thinking are good or bad for the people seldom concerns those trying to make their livings selling comics, novels, or films for mass consumption. They want their works to sell, and therefore they must tell readers what they want to hear. They must give their constituents stories that affirm the old values.

Sometimes it is difficult, but we must, on occasion, choose the world of art and forsake the world of play, of popular, easy, familiar old stories used by people who sell lots of fictions. Narrative artists explore the implications of values inherent in popular works, but with only a highly educated audience, often limited to the intellectual enclaves of universities. Narrative art may be acclaimed world wide by the few, but the many continue to read and look at what they like. Narrative art liberates readers from patterns which dominate the imaginations of the masses, but it only liberates those readers willing to give such narrative the serious attention it needs, those willing to play new games, willing to ignore old rules in order to make new discoveries about themselves and their societies.

Of course, scholars, critics, and other students of literature must continue to give serious literature the attention it requires, and must continue to encourage others to do the same. Still they may not—must not—be able to enforce their taste in reading upon the masses, in spite of required courses for graduation. They can, however, through attention to those works which make our familiar fictions unfamiliar, share with others those sometimes disturbing truths to be found in works of literary art.

At the same time they must also study that literature which is consumed by the masses in order to make more explicit the connections between popular narrative and human behavior, as well as between popular narrative and serious narrative art. Through the study of the ideology of mass entertainment they can enable others to discern what kind of dangers lurk behind the innocent appearing pages of the comic books on the newsstands. Although some literary scholars abhor the thought of a connection between the study of literature and the social sciences, a remark concerning the social sciences seem appropriate: "The social function of science vis-à-vis ideologies is first to understand them— what they are, how they work, what gives rise to them—and second to criticize them, to force them to come to terms with (but not necessarily to surrender to) reality" (Hunt 171, quoted from Clifford Geertz).

Frontier ideology continues to form the way we think about how we should relate to our New World neighbors and it is difficult, perhaps impossible, to completely eradicate such deeply embedded forms from our minds. Nevertheless, as one student of ideology in foreign policy has put it, "Though no historian can entirely rise above personal prejudice, success at illuminating the past depends in large measure on controlling those prejudices. Where (as here) the subject under scrutiny is a living body of ideas and assumptions, it is also necessary to achieve a degree of intellectual and emotional detachment—in effect, to see ideology as from a distance" (Hunt 173).

One way to achieve the necessary intellectual and emotional detachment will be through cross-cultural education. Anglo Americans must see how our national experience, and forms for apprehension, differ from those of other cultures. Through such education, we can begin to understand why all people in the world are not immediately willing and able to refashion themselves in exactly the pattern we provide. We can begin to see that, although other countries may not, especially in Latin America, have achieved the admirable democratic institutions we have achieved, they have perhaps maintained important family and religious traditions which better enable them to confront the terrors of our own country and time: drugs and crime.

Such cross-cultural education in Latin America might well enable people to modify their relationships with their governmental leaders so as to avoid the dependency, the subservience, and the subjugation associated with *caudillaje*. Perhaps through education and study of the problem people might choose a different, more humane form of government. In time, perhaps, Latin Americans will evolve a variant of their ideology which will give them the social and economic stability and justice everyone wants. Perhaps someday the majority of Latin American readers, not just their intellectuals and writers, will realize that the order provided by a *caudillo* or a *cacique* almost invariably carries with it a terrible price in lost human rights.

In time, and with education, Anglo American policy toward other countries might not be ruled by a frontier ideology that threatens to lead the United States into ugly wars with small, often poor, nations in Latin America—and elsewhere. However, today, in 1990, as we prepare to celebrate 500 years of European presence in the New World, *caudillos* rule in numerous Latin American countries, and the President of the United States and his advisers continue to ask for more and more money to maintain order in Central America.

No rigid pattern for the imagination should be allowed to dominate a culture. Yet as long as people only imagine that which has been imagined before, that which popular narrative sustains, then they will still be dominated by age old patterns which lead them, as Matiana said in *Las tierras flacas,* to repeat the same old mistakes. As long as the old stories, now given more powerful life through mass media, go unexamined, then people will think as the old stories teach them to think.

People do not have to be dominated by their fictions. Simply to recognize the way ideology can be conveyed by the stories we hear and read and see and to realize how that ideology can form a background for decisions about the way we conduct ourselves at home and abroad is to give ourselves the power to begin to make our own worlds over again. It is time for both Anglo and Latin American cultures to examine worn patterns for thought which have had so much to do with the contrasting ways the cultures have developed. Some aspects of those ideologic patterns should be saved, while others should be put aside to assure us a safe and just future.

Ultimately, the study of literature should help free us from our fictions.

Works Cited

Anderson, Thomas P. "The Social and Cultural Roots of Political Violence in Central America." *Aggressive Behavior* 2 (4) (1976): 249-255.

Arisso Thompson, Mercedes. "La imagen del caudillo en la novela hispanoamericana contemporanea." Diss. University of Colorado, 1977.

Asturias, Miguel Angel. *El Señor Presidente.* Trans. Frances Partridge. New York: Atheneum, 1969.

Autry, Gene. "Down Mexico Way" *Melody Ranch Theater.* Introd. Gene Autry and Pat Buttram. Dir. Ross Bagwell Jr. Prod. Ross Bagwell Sr. The Nashville Network, 14 September 1987.

———— *Melody Ranch Theater.* Introd. Gene Autry and Pat Buttram. Dir. Ross Bagwell Jr. Prod. Ross Bagwell Sr. The Nashville Network. 21 August 1987.

———— *Melody Ranch Theater.* Introd. Gene Autry and Pat Buttram. Dir. Ross Bagwell Jr. Prod. Ross Bagwell Sr. The Nashville Network, 1 September 1987.

———— "Rancho Grande" Dir. Frank McDonald. Prod. William Berke. Screenplay: Bradford Ropes, Betty Burbridge, and Peter Miline, based on an original story by Peter Miline and Connie Lee.

———— "Twilight on the Rio Grande" Magill's Survey of Cinema, Dialog Information Retrieval Services, 1 September 1987.

Ayala Blanco, Jorge. *Aventura del cine Mexicano.* Mexico City: Ediciones Era, S.A., 1968.

Barron, James. "Author Louis L'Amour Dies at 80; Chronicler of the American West." *New York Times.* 13 June 1988, natl. ed.: 16.

Berger, Thomas. *Little Big Man.* New York: Fawcett World Library, 1964.

"Boots and Saddles" Writ. Jack Nettleford and Olive Drake. *Melody Ranch Theater.* Introd. Gene Autry and Pat Buttram. Dir. Ross Bagwell Jr. Prod. Ross Bagwell Sr. The Nashville Network. 17 August 1987.

Branch, E. Douglas. *Westward: The Romance of the American Frontier.* 1930. New York: Cooper Square Publishers, Inc., 1969.

Bunge, Carlos Octavio. *Nuestra América: ensayo de psicologia social.* 6th ed. Buenos Aires: Casa Vaccaro, 1918. Excerpted and reprinted in *Dictatorship in Spanish America.* Ed. and Introd. by Hugh M. Hamill, Jr. New York: Alfred A. Knopf, 1965, pp. 120-124.

Chevalier, Francois. " 'Caudillos' et 'caciques' en Amérique: contribution à l'étude des liens personnels." *Mélanges offerts à Marcel Bataillon par les Hispanistes Francais,* a special issue of *Bulletin Hispanique,* Vol. LXIV bis (1962), pp. 30-47. Translated and reprinted in part as "The Roots of Personalismo," in *Dictatorship in Spanish America,* ed. and introd. by Hugh M. Hamill, Jr. New York: Alfred A. Knopf, 1965.

Clark, Walter Van Tilburg. *The Ox-Bow Incident.* New York: Random House, 1940.

Columbus, Christopher. *Four Voyages to the New World.* Trans. and Ed. R.H. Major. Gloucester, Massachusetts: Peter Smith, 1978.

de la Mare, Walter. *Desert Islands and Robinson Crusoe*. London: Faber and Faber, 1930.

del Rio, Eduardo. *Los Dictaduros: El Militarismo en América Latina*. Mexico City: Editorial Nueva Imagen, 1982.

———— *Los agachados*, "*Viven mas gringos en mexico que braceros en ee.uu.*" año VIII, num 248, March, 1976.

———— *Los agachados*, "Otra industria sin chimeneas: los braceros." año V, num. 173, 16 octubre 1974.

Doctorow, D.L. *Welcome to Hard Times*. New York: Simon and Schuster, Inc., 1960.

Eco, Umberto. *Apocalipticos e integrados ante la cultura de las masas*. Barcelona: Editorial Lumen, 1968.

"El cacique," *El Goleador Misterioso*, año 1, no. 40, 4 de junio de 1974.

Ellul, Jacques. *The Humiliation of the Word*. Trans. Joyce Main Hanks. Grand Rapids, Michigan: William B. Eerdmans Publishing Company, 1985.

Estefanía, M.L. *De Dodge City a Abilene*. Barcelone: Editorial Bruguera, 1963.

———— *El final del indio apache*. Madrid: Editorial Andina, S.A. 1980.

———— *¡Es una india!*. Madrid. Editorial Andina, S.A., 1981.

———— *La leyenda de un fraile*. Bardelona: Editorial Bruguera, S.A., 1963.

———— *Sangre junto al rio*. Barcelona: Editorial Bruguera, S.A., 1977.

———— *¿También los cuatreros?*. Madrid: Editorial Andina, 1980.

Everson, William K. *A Pictorial History of the Western Film*. New York: The Citadel Press, 1969.

Fenin, George N. and William K. Everson. *The Western, from silents to the seventies*. Rev. ed. Harmondsworth, Middlesex, England: Penguin Books Ltd., 1977.

Fitzgibbon, Russel H. " '*Continuismo*' " in Central America and the Caribbean," *The Inter-American Quarterly*, Vol. II (July, 1940), p. 56-74. Excerpted and reprinted in *Dictatorship in Spanish America*. Ed. and Introd. by Hugh M. Hamill, Jr. New York: Alfred A. Knopf, 1965, pp. 145-154.

Folsom, James K. *The American Western Novel*. New Haven, Connecticut: College and University Press, 1966.

Hamill, Hugh M. Introduction. *Dictatorship in Spanish America*. ed. and introd. by Hugh M. Hamill. New York: Alfred A. Knopf. 1965. 3-25.

Hanke, Lewis. *All Mankind is One*. Dekalb: Northern Illinois University Press, 1974.

Hardy, Phil. *The Western*. New York: William Morrow and Company, Inc. 1983.

Hennessy, Alistair. *The Frontier in Latin American History*. Albuquerque: University of New Mexico Press, 1978.

Henriquez Ureña, Pedro. *A Concise History of Latin American Culture*. Translated and with a Supplementary Chapter by Gilbert Chase. New York: Frederick A. Praeger, 1966.

Hinds, Harold E. Jr., "Comics: Introduction." *Studies in Latin American Popular Culture* 4 (1985): 1-32.

Horwitz, James. *They Went Thataway*. New York: Ballantine Books, 1976.

Hunt, Michael H. *Ideology and U.S. Foreign Policy*. New Haven and London: Yale University Press, 1987.

Jameson, Fredric. *The Prison House of Language*. Princeton, N.J.: Princeton University Press, 1972.

L'Amour, Louis. *Kiowa Trail*. Toronto: Bantam Books, 1964.

———— *Ride the Dark Trail*. Toronto: Bantam Books, 1972.

———— *Sackett*. Toronto: Bantam Books, 1961.

———— *Shalako*. Toronto: Bantam Books, 1962.

_____ *The Californios*. Toronto: Bantam Books, 1974.

_____ *The Daybreakers*. Toronto: Bantam Books, 1960.

_____ *The Lonesome Gods*. Toronto: Bantam Books, 1983.

_____ *The Man Called Noon*. Toronto: Bantam Books, 1970.

_____ *The Sackett Brand*. Toronto: Bantam Books, 1965.

_____ *Treasure Mountain*. Toronto: Bantam Books, 1972.

Lloyd Jones, Chester. *Guatemala: Past and Present*. Minneapolis: University of Minnesota Press, 1940, pp. 339, 343-350, 351-356. Excerpted and reprinted in *Dictatorship in Spanish America*. Ed. and Introd. by Hugh M. Hamill, Jr. New York: Alfred E. Knopf, Inc., pp. 221-234.

Madariaga, Salvador de. "Man and the Universe in Spain." *Spain: a Modern History*. New York: Frederick A. Praeger, Inc., 1958. Pages 17-18 and 20-23 are reprinted in *Dictatorship in Spanish America*. ed. and introd. by Hugh M. Hamill, Jr. New York: Alfred A. Knopf, 1965.

Mañach, Jorge. *Teoria de la frontera*. Introd. Concha Meléndez. Rio Piedras. Puerto Rico: Editorial Universitaria, 1970.

Marcus, Steven. *The Other Victorians*. New York: Basic Books, 1966.

"Mexicali Rose" Writ. Jack Nettleford and Olive Drake. *Melody Ranch Theater*. Introd. Gene Autry and Pat Buttram. Dir. Ross Bagwell Jr. Prod. Ross Bagwell Sr. The Nashville Network. 24 August 1987.

Miller, Lee O. *The Great Cowboy Stars of Movies and Television*. Introd. Joel McCrea. Westport, Connecticut: Arlington House Publishers, 1979.

Mora, Carl J. *Mexican Cinema: Reflections of a Society, 1896-1980*. Berkeley: University of California Press, 1982.

Morse, Robert M. "Toward a Theory of Spanish American Government," *Journal of the History of Ideas*, Vol. XV (1954), pp. 71-93. Excerpts reprinted in *Dictatorship in Spanish America*, ed. and introd. by Hugh M. Hamill, Jr. New York: Alfred A. Knopf, 1965, pp. 52-68.

Navarro, Rafael C. and Modesto Vasquez. *Aguila Solitaria*. Bogata: Editora Cinco S.A., 1979.

O'Gorman, Edmundo. *La invencion de América: El universalismo de la Culture de Occidente* (Mexico—Buenos Aires: Fondo de Cultura Economica, 1958).

Ovejero, Gregorio. Letter to the author. 8 December 1980.

Oxford English Dictionary, Vol. II, 1970 ed.

Paz, Octavio. *The Labyrinth of Solitude: Life and Thought in Mexico*. Trans. Lysander Kemp. New York: Grove Press, Inc. 1969.

Ramsaye, Terry. *A Million and One Nights: A History of the Motion Picture*. New York: Simon and Schuster, 1926.

Rangel, Carlos. *Del buen salvajee al buen revolucionario*. Caracas: Monte Ovila Editores, S.A., 1976.

Sarmiento, Domingo F. *Facundo: Civilizacion y Barbarie*. Seventh Edition. Buenos Aires: Espasa-Calpe Argentina, S.A. 1967.

Schaefer, Jack. *Shane*. 1949. Boston: Houghton Mifflin Company, 1979.

Slotkin, Richard. *Regeneration Through Violence: The Mythology of the American Frontier, 1600-1860*. Middletown, Connecticut: Wesleyan University Press, 1973.

Smith, Henry Nash. 1950. *Virgin Land: The American West as Symbol and Myth*. 2nd ed. Cambridge, Massachusetts and London, England: Harvard University Press, 1970.

Strong, Josiah. *Our Country*. New York, 1885. Quoted in Hunt, Michael H. *Ideology and U.S. Foreign Policy*. New Haven and London: Yale University Press, 1987.

Tucker, Frank H. *The Frontier Spirit and Progress*. Chicago: Nelson-Hall, 1980. Tucker paraphrases from Sam J. Junwall's book, *Science Fiction: What It's All About*. New York: 1971.

Turner, F.J. "Contributions of the West to American Democracy." *Selected Essays of Frederick Jackson Turner*. Ed. R.A. Billington. Englewood Cliffs: Prentice, 1961.

Vargas Llosa, Mario. *The Green House*. Trans. Gregory Rabassa. New York: Harper & Row, Publishers, 1968.

Warshow, Robert. "The Gangster as Tragic Hero." *The Popular Arts in America: A Reader*. Ed. William M. Hammel. New York: Harcourt Brace Jovanovich, Inc. 1972.

Wolf, Eric R., and Edward C. Hansen. *The Human Condition in Latin America*. New York: Oxford University Press, 1972.

Wright, Will. *Six Guns and Society: A Structural Study of the Western*. Berkeley: University of California Press, 1975.

Yáñez, Agustin. *The Lean Lands*. Trans. Ethel Brinton. Austin: University of Texas Press, 1968.

Zea, Leopoldo. *América en la historia*. (Mexico—Buenos Aires: Fondo de Cultura Economica, 1957).

Index